M000307989

LEADING

IDENTITY

Journey to Your Purposeful Identity &
Become a True, Fulfilled, and Lasting
Leader

Emmitt A. Savannah III

LEADING IDENTITY
Journey to Your Purposeful Identity & Become a
True, Fulfilled, and Lasting Leader

by

Emmitt A. Savannah III

Copyright © 2021

ISBN: 978-1-7373992-1-6

Dedication

I would like to dedicate this book to my darling wife, Alethea. You have been a part of my journey and seen the good, the bad, and the ugly. Your support, prayers, and love have encouraged me and inspired me to keep going. I love you tremendously and am ever so grateful for you. Life is so much better with you in it. I could not have accomplished writing this book without you.

Acknowledgments

I would like to thank:
- My wife, Alethea, who has been there and encouraged me every step of the way.
- My mom.
- My dad.
- My brother.
- My sister.
- David and Jennifer Dillman.
- Dennis and Phyllis Scheminske.
- Chris and Kacee Pate.
- Joseph Kreeb.
- My family.
- My friends who know who they are.
- My entire publishing team.
- Most of all, I want to thank God for His grace that allowed this book to come to fruition.

Preface

This book has been a long time coming, and the subject matter is near and dear to my heart. As I have continued to grow in my career, I have undoubtedly had a strong sense of connection with people and want to see them blossom and flourish not only in the workplace, but also in life. It took me some years to first begin to understand myself and how I think, and then harness that in a way that influenced how I live and work with others.

This book will appeal to most anyone who has a heart for people and a desire to lead more effectively, whether it be in the workplace, at home, or merely leading yourself. However, I have gone a bit beyond just "one who has a heart for people and a desire to lead more effectively." Something deeper is at play, and not exploring that depth would make this book just another shallow, though practical, self-help book to check off your list in hopes of gathering some nugget of wisdom before moving on to the next book or podcast.

This book is aimed toward those who are currently struggling to find purpose, or who have already found a sense of purpose, are at the very start of their career, at the top executive level of leadership, or anywhere in between. No matter where you work and lead, I've come to realize that one main factor determines how you work, lead, live, and treat others—that is knowing your *identity*.

First, let me be quite clear about what I don't mean by that. In today's culture, the word *identity* has a wide variety of meanings; so I want to clarify my definition of the word. I am not referring to gender identity, so my definition may turn you away or intrigue you all the more. My goal is not to purposely exclude anyone, but rather bring understanding from a perspective you may not have considered, and the realization that whether you agree with me or not, identity inarguably has an impact on how you live, lead, and interact with others. So, I challenge you to approach the topic of identity with an open mind as I attempt to inspire you.

Speaking from experience, you cannot have leadership apart from identity. The two are intertwined like words on a page or art on a canvas. A blank page or canvas is nothing worthy of observation. A beautiful canvas with horrible art is not enticing either. The canvas or page represents your leadership area and position. Everyone has leadership areas where they are expected to write and paint. In other words, you are expected to leave an imprint, an impression, or make a difference from what once was with the hope to influence and inspire. Perhaps your hope is just to effect change or simply get the job done without the consideration or awareness of influencing and inspiring, depending on your default leadership style. However, whatever you write or paint on that leadership canvas *starts* with your identity.

The observations in this book are based on both my own and others' evaluated experiences, wisdom gleaned from others, knowledge amassed from various sources and people, conversations with various leaders in both corporate and religious settings, and my weighed and analyzed personal convictions from my Christian faith.

Without exception, every one places belief, faith or confidence—our hope and trust—in something or someone; and we both consciously and subconsciously build relationship with that very thing or what embodies it, which we hold in high esteem. Those terms can be combined into three; Belief, Expectation (faith and hope), and Trust: your B.E.T. You effectively put your BET in what you have looked at, studied, come to understand, and are persuaded to stand by and stand up for, regardless of what it is.

My purpose in writing is not to try to convince others to convert to any religious faith or denomination. I am merely stating the fact that I am a Christian so that you understand this is a part of who I am, part of my identity, which is the very premise and idea of the book: to understand who or what you see yourself as and how that impacts the way you lead others, yourself, and your family. In light of that, I'd be foolish to leave out that information about myself. Whether you are a Christian or not, the person of Jesus— whom I reference in this book—when considered from an objective point of view, proved to be knowledgeable, wise, purpose-driven, and one of the best examples, if not *the* best historical example, of a world-changing leader and influencer as He dealt with the issue of identity within Himself and others.

Identity is a question of who you are that can be found in what you trust, what you see yourself belonging to, your perceived purpose as to why you are here, and what you are competent in doing.

Contents

1

INTRODUCTION

I've battled thoughts of not having anything worthy to say, not being smart enough, belittling what I have learned, and thinking that I am not respectable enough for others to glean from what I have to impart to them. Can you relate? This kind of thinking is rooted and grounded in lies I believed about myself for years. Everything I just stated has been a part of how I have viewed myself and how I have felt others viewed me, which resulted in the building blocks of my identity. I want to address that very issue. This book came about after battling internal struggles when an ever-growing and developing passion and determination for leading and developing others began to outweigh my challenges. The identity I took on for so long—which was rooted in lies I believed about myself—hindered me from leading the way I should have during the earlier parts of my career as both a frontline employee and in leadership-management positions. Even more, it affected the way I led my wife and children.

So many in our society, both young and old, face this issue. Regardless of age, many people struggle to figure out who they are, tend to intentionally bend to meet societal expectations, and can often forsake their identities to fit in, be accepted, or obtain power and wealth, due to being enamored with the societal and secular idea of success. This continues to blur the image of who they are, and when identity is rooted in things so temporal, compromising, vulnerable, and shifting, the leader inside them reflects this instability.

I wrote a journal entry on February 4, 2020, after having read 1 Thessalonians 4:1-8. In these verses, a man named Paul illustrates the way to walk and please God. He further impresses on the audience's heart what the will of God is for them: that they abstain from sexual immorality and control their bodies in holiness and honor to make them available for God's purpose and separate them from the profane.

As I pondered this, I thought about what identity has to do with this. Does what you follow reveal what you like to connect with? Is it something you identify with? I most definitely would. I think of who or what I follow on Instagram. I Thessalonians 4:1 (AMP) uses the phrase "that you follow the instruction." Again, following something, in most cases, means you agree with it, like it, want it, or want to emulate it in some way, and is associated with your identity—though not a hundred percent of the time. When this is not the case, for example, I may follow something or someone I'm not in agreement with because I want to hear and understand opposing arguments to help me better articulate my position and connect with understanding with others who have opposing points of view.

The issue of identity and leadership is not just a quick one-stop shop. It takes some introspection. This book will take you on a bit of that journey, and I am being vulnerable to share my journey with you, offering implications and applications that you can employ. First, you need awareness and understanding of what your identity is in. Once you understand that, then you will have the ability to better align or realign the character and actions that will determine the depth, impact, and duration of your success.

If you desire to get started on that journey of becoming a better and more focused leader, and having a better sense of why this is such a critical topic that is often ignored and inadequately addressed, and helping you awaken a solid leader within because of a solid identity, then this book is for you. Don't delay! What I discovered was not only life-changing but also literally life-saving. It can be for you as well.

2

THE IDENTITY JOURNEY BEGINS

Identity is a question of who you are that can be found in what you trust, what you see yourself belonging to, your perceived purpose as to why you are here, and where your competencies lie.

Until I was five years old, I lived in a happy and loving home, from my perspective; however much of that is clouded in my memory due to events that were singed in my brain, mostly due to lack of understanding and shock due to being just a toddler. I have two older siblings. Based on stories we have shared over the years, all three of us have very different perspectives of our childhood.

My parents divorced when I was around five years old. I remember some details of the events of the day my parents split and how ugly and surreal that moment seemed to me. I remember just standing still, in shock. While I did not understand fully what was happening, I knew that my parents would never be the same and life as I knew it would change forever. I had no idea how to face the days ahead. Even though I was small in stature, that was the first time I felt insignificant, though I had no clue what that word even meant at the time. Words like *insignificant* are not exactly in a five year old's vocabulary, but it is a feeling I have struggled with for years, even to this day at times. That was a significant turning point in my character building, in the shaping of my personality, in what and who I would trust, in how I would think, in how I interacted with my parents and others, and even how I would relate to God. Obviously, none of that was going through my head at that age. At that point, I was just trying to make sense of what had happened and wondered if I would ever see my parents together again.

From that point until I was about ten, I grew used to the fact that I lived in a single-parent household. I gave up wishing for my parents to get back together. After all of the legal mumbo jumbo my parents went through after the divorce, I got to see my dad every other weekend and entirely during the summer months. My older siblings had a different father than I, so the legal custody and visitation rights really concerned only me, I assume; but it was quite difficult to constantly adjust and readjust to new settings that were constantly changing, from one home to another, from one set of customs to another. I lived in two different worlds, with two parents that had different values, views, ideologies, philosophies, parenting styles, religious perspectives, and very different ways of interacting with me. These two worlds seemed to clash often, and I was caught in the middle. I felt like I was in between two clanging cymbals, left only with the ringing sound in my ears. It was overwhelming to say the least, and no one else knew or understood what I was going through.

When I was about ten, my dad would take me on trips in the summer months. These were some exciting times. I got to see all sorts of things like mountains and animals in the wilderness that a child would normally see only in zoos. We went hiking, camping, fishing, river tubing, rafting, and on all sorts of fun activities. These trips took my mind off of the uncomfortable feeling that I was being ripped away from and stripped of what was important to me and bombarded with situations I had to try to analyze the best I could, then make the decisions I was expected to make. Those expectations differed from one household to the other. However, during these trips with dad, I looked forward to the next adventure, the next day, the thrill of sleeping in our tent and hearing strange sounds as I lay awake at night while my dad slept. It was a captivating time and experience for me.

My dad and I visited several national parks and historical monuments. He has always been a history buff and wanted me to know my ancestral as well as general history. It was important to him because he felt having knowledge of ancient and ancestral history, well beyond and before slavery, would plant positive thoughts of what I could achieve in life.

When I would return home to live with mom and my siblings, I was more and more reluctant to tell them of the experiences I had over the years on those trips because I knew my siblings did not experience that, and I did not want them to feel bad about that. Being torn between two worlds, I felt a great sense of compassion for my siblings as well as others. I realized that despite my messed-up situation, I was still able to experience some positives that others didn't get to experience, and this quickly helped me to realize that bragging only created enemies, not friends. So, I stayed quiet about what we did and only told about it when I was directly asked.

During this same time—my elementary years—I did not have many friends. I did grow very close to two guys, though, one of whom was in my wedding years later, and we kept in touch for quite some time. But I found it hard to relate to others at this age. I felt different. I thought differently. I would begin to analyze people to see if they would be worth a friendship based on how they behaved, and I then analyzed and tried to predict the longevity of that potential friendship. I did this because I feared feeling insignificant, the way I had when my parents split. See how that single event began to shape how I interacted with others? I did not trust others much at all at this age, but I didn't like the feeling of being excluded; so, I tried the best I could to fit in. I would do things to get approval from my peers just to be included, even though I might not have thought much of them at the time. I rarely regarded anyone as a friend.

During my middle school years, from the ages of eleven to fifteen, my body was going through a lot of hormonal changes, and I was not ready. No one warned me; no one talked to me about what would be happening in my body over these years. As for almost any kid, middle school was a culture shock with so many kids of different nationalities, religions, cultures, and styles, not to mention so many girls and the issues that come with that for young boys at that age. In addition, I had many more responsibilities but also much more freedom at the same time. Coming from an elementary school where I mainly saw the same few kids every day and then going into middle school where there were somewhere around 1,000 students, I felt quite overwhelmed. I am naturally an introvert, so entering a school of this size felt daunting and overwhelming.

At this age, I was trying to make sense of many of my thoughts, emotions, and feelings. I was mostly quiet and kept to myself, other than the few classmates I regularly encountered and started to connect with.

I began to form a strong bond with a boy I will refer to as Dem. I had never met anyone like him. He seemed to be everything I wanted to be but was not. He was charming, outgoing, outspoken, had a jovial demeanor and such a friendly and warm personality. When he talked with you, he was always smiling, and you felt significant, seen and valued as a person. Even teachers enjoyed talking with him and having him as a student in their classes. He was well mannered, respectful, and liked to have fun.

Of course, we still participated in all the goofiness, foolishness and awkwardness that just comes with that age. On our last day of middle school, we snuck up on the school roof and ran around a bit just because it seemed like an exhilarating thing to do. I never would have thought to do something like that. I have never even told anyone about that until writing this book.

Dem and I also decided to participate in sports together, like wrestling and track. Again, those are activities I probably never would have taken up on my own, but Dem helped bring out a different side of me because he was someone I felt comfortable around. At the time, unbeknownst to me, I was experiencing a newfound sense of belonging, acceptance, approval, assurance, and even a sense of security in who I was and wanted to become. I didn't know anyone at our school who didn't like Dem. Looking back, I believe this is why he made such an impression on me. He was one of the first people I ever met, outside of my family, that made me feel significant and valued as a person. We began forming a trusted bond and friendship, and he was one of the few people I could open up to and be myself around. I really admired him and valued our friendship, and though I did not realize it at the time, this was a turning point in my life. It significantly began to shape how I viewed myself and came to know more of my own identity.

I entered high school at fifteen, and this was yet another new environment for me. Most of my friends in middle school went to another high school, so I knew no one at my new school. I began the school year as a very quiet and shy person, yet more observant and analytical of those around me. You can likely conclude by now that I was not the most popular person, nor did I intend to be. Large crowds and even a large amount of attention was something I wanted to avoid. With my analytical skills and keen observation of people, I could ascertain if someone would be a good influence on me or if I could be a positive influence on them. I was intentional about building relationships with only a select few people. I was more sure of myself in high school than ever, but I still had a significant number of insecurities that I hadn't dealt with.

My high school had a smaller student body population than middle school, so it didn't feel quite so overwhelming to me. It was also a magnet school that you had to test into, so the curriculum was heavy on the academic side. We had no sports, and many of the students were very smart top performers. The school's emphasis and specialty was on health professions. Entire programs and classes were geared to enable students to delve into the medical and health professional world. It was challenging and provided so much opportunity and growth; I loved the challenge and, even more so, I loved that fact I didn't have to deal much with some of the typical issues many encounter in larger high schools in urban areas.

It was during my high school years that I began to think about my future more and more. College was rapidly approaching, and I was expected to know what I wanted to do for the rest of my life when it arrived. I also grew more intellectually in my faith as a Christian during high school. In light of that, I thought I should start thinking about who my future wife would be and trying to be a strong leader and strong man of faith. During these years, I could most likely have been described as tender-hearted, compassionate, quiet, observant, analytical, responsible, kind, and accepting of others; yet, I was insecure and unsure of who or what I wanted to be. This uncertainty created havoc in my mind because I still found myself wanting to fit in and bend a little bit for acceptance.

I became infatuated with one particular girl who I will leave nameless, and we developed an exclusive relationship throughout most of our high school years. By my junior year of high school, I thought I would marry her. However, when our relationship grew rocky, unstable, and unhealthy, I found myself compromising my integrity and justifying it internally just to remain with her. After high school, she and I went to different colleges in different states, and I had a strong feeling that our relationship would not last beyond our freshman year of college. I thought because she was going to what many of my peers identified as a "party school" where she would be bombarded with a bunch of immature, hormonal, and sexually driven guys that would be more appealing to her than I was, that our relationship would quickly dissolve. And it did just that. Though I anticipated that happening, it still left me with feelings of despair and that, somehow, I was not good enough. I felt that I had failed in this area of my life. It was a devastating blow to my confidence, to my faith, to how I viewed myself, and to a large part of my identity.

When I went to college at eighteen, I soon joined my girlfriend's home church. I really enjoyed the people there, and it somehow made me feel closer to her because I was connecting to the same people she was close to. Still, the day before finals began after our freshman year ended, she broke off the relationship over the phone. Though I had felt it was coming, I was both surprised and devastated. For the very first time, I was defeated by thoughts that I couldn't measure up and was insignificant to her. It was a devastating blow to my confidence, and I lost the sense of who I was at that moment.

It was hard to study, sleep, focus and engage with people fully—even my family. I found it difficult to trust people, most of all women. The breakup started a downward spiral for me in how I viewed women, relationships, and even myself. I decided it was better not to get serious with anyone ever again and to avoid marriage. I failed to see that I was also not serious with myself. I entered a place of increasing insecurity, constantly feeling like a failure, and I struggled with that identity issue throughout much of my adult life.

As the months passed, my heartache healed. I was experiencing so much that was new for me, including new freedoms I never had before. However, I was also under a tremendous amount of pressure due to expectations that I'd determine a career path soon. Growing up, I aspired to be just one thing—an astronaut. Once I reached college, I no longer had that desire, plus I quickly realized I was not smart enough. My dad really wanted me to be a doctor, so I chose ophthalmology since it seemed lucrative enough; still, I wasn't passionate about it, despite making efforts to set up a path to get into med school. I'd had the opportunity during high school to work alongside an ophthalmologist to observe the practice, so I began forcing myself to take more of an interest in the anatomy of the human eye.

At one point in college, I asked myself what I truly enjoyed. Two things came to mind: to this day, music and snakes top my list. I considered changing to the music program and studying herpetology. I even emailed Jack Hanna's team seeking an internship at the zoo he worked out of. I decided to be one of those animal enthusiasts you saw on tv, just like Jack Hanna. My dad quickly shot down that idea. Back at square one, I was fearful about my future, feeling like a failure, with no prospects of doing anything meaningful with my life.

As a biology student, it seemed my only two options were either med school or teaching biology. I had no desire to do either, so I felt stuck. I didn't think I was smart enough to be a doctor because my self-confidence was shot, and I did not want to be a teacher because I always heard they didn't make enough money. I also did not want to spend the next ten plus years of my life studying medicine, but I thought I'd be up for the challenge if I convinced myself I wanted to be an ophthalmologist. So, I headed once again in the direction of that goal, but the passion just faded over time. I felt so lost.

While sorting out these career decisions, my broken heart didn't prevent me from dating. While not looking for a serious relationship, deep down, I still had a spark of desire to find a good woman. I dated a few women with whom I could engage intellectually as well have a bit of fun just enjoying life, as much as a college student's limited funds would allow. I was not taking either myself or any relationship too seriously during this time, but I was also gauging whether one of these relationships could end up going somewhere beyond college.

Growing Up

After my parents' divorce, I primarily lived in a low-income, single-parent household; but I was still being raised by both parents, yet in very different environments. It began to feel like I was living two separate lives, with two of nearly everything. Some good came of that from a kid's perspective—like having two Christmases, two Thanksgivings, two birthday parties, etc. But while that was fun, it never outweighed the burdens and emotional turmoil I wrestled with that my family knew nothing about.

A lot of my early memories are shadowed by brutal events. I recall, at the age of seven or so, seeing my dad hit over the head with a bat by one of my uncles, one of my mom's brothers, because of an altercation my dad had with my mom. I saw my mom rush him to the hospital. I remember the driveway being full of blood, as I watched in shock and wondered if I'd ever see my dad again. When I was about ten, one of my uncles took me outside, told me to tighten my abs, and then punched me in the stomach repeatedly, as they do in martial arts, to "toughen me up." I was often referred to as skinny and weak and was picked on by people in my mom's family as well as people at school during my adolescent years. I never experienced any of that with dad's family.

Because of these experiences, I lived in a state of constant tension between my two families. I wanted everyone's approval, so I resolved to try to be perfect, keep quiet, and give no one any reason to disapprove of me. But anytime I did what Dad considered unfavorable, even years after my parents' divorce, he would say, "That's the McDaniel in you. You're a Savannah!" My siblings, who have a different father than I, also have the last name McDaniel. When dad said that, I'd cringe; but it also reinforced the idea that I was supposed to be better than my mom's side of the family because I carried the last name Savannah. I began to inwardly think that the Savannah side of me was better, and so I carried a false sense of pride because of my last name. This notion only reinforced the idea that I had to aspire to perfection. It was not healthy, and it was not right, but I didn't realize any of that at the time. I was simply caught in this web of conflict that I had no idea how to navigate from the time my parents divorced until I was in college.

Before I move on, it's only fair to acknowledge that my childhood was not an entirely negative experience. Both our positive and negative experiences influence our identity and character development. While the negatives ones are significant, the positive ones can have just as much significance, if not more, if we choose to let them. For me, the positive experiences have had a much more profound impact on me than the negative ones.

Coming up in a single-parent household, I developed a deep connection with my mother. She has always felt like a safe place for me, and her opinion of me influenced me over anyone else's; but it doesn't mean other people's opinion did not affect me. My mom is a very spiritual person still to this day, one who I have always regarded as loving, compassionate, giving, faithful, and strong. I have seen her resolve in very difficult situations and how her faith in God strengthened her. As a child, observing this in my mother made me admire her and want to emulate what I saw in her life. Both sides of my family are predominantly Christian, so I was influenced on both sides to pursue the Christian faith, but she influenced me more than anyone else to pursue and understand more about God and Christianity.

I also developed a deep and close bond with my paternal grandparents. My dad's siblings, their children (my cousins), and much of my paternal extended family lived in the Dallas-Fort Worth area, so we would visit often every summer and on extended weekends sometimes. My grandparents affected me profoundly. For one, they were the only couple I knew who had been married fifty plus years. Because I was from a broken home with a single maternal grandmother, they were my opportunity to see firsthand what a lasting marriage was like. They were my only example of a seasoned, healthy marriage, and they seemed happy and content. In fact, the guidance and words of wisdom and example that I received from all of my grandparents were a bucket of gold in my eyes.

My paternal grandparents were everything I wanted to be. I felt loved and protected when I was them. They used seemingly insignificant moments to teach me by way of example, story, and reference. When I would go out with my grandmother, she would teach me how to be a gentleman. My grandfather led humbly and quietly. He was not an outspoken person, but his words carried weight and were never wasted. I deeply admired that about him; anyone who knows me knows that I, too, am a man of few words and a reserved personality. My grandparents were Christians who faithfully served in their local church. Everyone seemed to love my grandfather and grandmother. I longed to be like them.

Overall, I had a happy childhood, despite the negatives that came with life. I got along with my siblings well. We were there for each other and respected each other. My brother, Chris, the oldest, did his best and did well leading my sister and me. With no father in the home, he was the male head and leader for us. He was expected to lead by example, and he did just that. We had our moments of tension and disagreements as brothers do, but by and large, he has been nothing but an amazing brother and example to emulate. He did well in school, and I never recall him ever getting into serious trouble. He was a model student, and I knew he would end up well-positioned in life. He is now an accomplished architect.

Without his father in his life, Chris was significantly influenced by my mom's brothers, his uncles. They were his father-figures. My brother and I had very different "dad" experiences growing up, and so he wrestled with situations that I did not experience; but I tried to understand.

I felt at peace at home with my siblings and mother. We didn't fight or argue, and we were never a loud family. Yes, there were moments of disagreements and misunderstandings, but it never resulted in anyone lashing out. We respected one another. It was ingrained in us to treat our family and others with respect. When I witnessed other families arguing or fighting, it seemed so bizarre and confusing to me when I was a child.

My sister, Shae, and I also had a unique relationship. She and I were closer in age as she is the middle child. We played together and poked fun at each other growing up. My sister was the fun-loving one. She made our growing up years fun and exciting. She was another safe place for me as she took my mind off of the negative emotional and relational fluctuations I experienced as a child. With her, all the struggles just went away for a while, and I was in this perfect place of peace, joy, and fun. Even to this day, she reminds me of that as we still have that kind of playful and jovial interactions when we're around each other. We still poke fun at each other like we did when were kids, even though we're both married and now have children of our own. She is an amazing sister and friend, and I could not imagine what my childhood would have been like without her.

Growing up, I was always in my own head, thinking, analyzing, rationalizing, trying to make sense of who I was in a world that seemed too much to handle and too confusing to understand. I did not know how to put words to it then, but I was just trying to figure out my identity. I lived in two different worlds at the same time, and I feared life would be confusing for the rest of my life. As I grew older, I became more quiet, more reserved, more tender-hearted, and listened three times more than I talked—partly because I was unsure of what to say much of the time. I was constantly trying to make sense of my world. I would often become mentally and emotionally exhausted with it all, so I looked for vices to escape my reality. This is where college became interesting for me.

I went to the University of Houston, so I stayed close to home. My freshman year of college, even though I was still in Houston, which is where my family lived, I lived on campus. I majored in biology and minored in health, thinking I would go on to medical school and become the doctor my father aspired for me to be. I wanted to make him proud. Initially, I decided that any social life would be non-existent because I was supposed to study hard, make good grades, get into medical school and fully walk into my calling in life and embody the "golden-child" standard that I felt had been placed on me.

I mention the golden-child standard because this is what I functionally believed I had to live up to based on what was reinforced to me growing up. You see, what much of my family saw on the external and often verbally recognized in an affirming tone was that I was well-mannered, wise beyond my years, intelligent, cogitative, talented, accomplished, and a nice Christian boy who would be an even stronger Christian man. I believed them.

In my senior year of high school, I felt a strong inclination to become a preacher of the gospel. This was the icing on the cake for my family. My family could not have been prouder once I announced this, and they were made even more proud once I preached my first sermon. Externally, I looked perfect on the outside, as if everything came easily; this image kept me from sinking into the mental and emotional turmoil that constantly tried to peek out from underneath.

Realistically, I did not feel at all "golden." I just felt that as long as others were approving of me, then everything was okay; so this approval became part of my purpose and identity. It was what I ascribed the most worth to because it was what sustained me while at the same time causing me the most anxiety. It's sort of like sugar. It might perk you up and make you feel good for a while, but when you keep eating it, it comes up short of providing the necessary nutrients for your body; eventually, you start feeling the devastating effects.

However, while many of my mannerisms and personality were very much true to who I was, I never took time to consider who I wanted to become for myself. I was allowing others' approval and satisfaction of what was pleasing to them to dictate what I was deciding to become and do. After years of this, it was beating me down emotionally and psychologically. The inner turmoil and torment was unbearable, but I did not know what to do, how to fix it, how to change, or even how to articulate this to anyone; so I kept right on the path I was on and ran on the fumes of the accolades I received from family and friends. Even when I desperately wanted to talk about this, I thought it would ruin the image my family had of me, so I quickly tossed out that idea. I kept trying to use my wits to figure it out on my own...and the more I heard and received the accolades from my family, the better I felt.

Another escape for me was women. In college, I had two focuses—work and relationships. Relationships with people that approved of me were sort of life-giving, so this is what I started to seek out in women. I thought if I could develop an ongoing relationship with a girl to whom I was attracted, I would receive a constant bombardment of approval. Over time, I developed a very unhealthy view of women because they were serving only to meet an inner need and pacify my inner turmoil, although they did not realize it. I interpreted their time and attention to me as approval, and I was living off of that fuel. It was even better than my family giving me a pat on the back. Being relationally involved and having that reinforced with physical touch was the strongest sensation of approval I could find, so I kept at it. However, I would find myself devastated each time a woman would end our association—my world would crash and spiral out of control. It was one of the most unbearable feelings because I felt hopelessness, but was forced to find my fix in someone else. But it kept ending the same way, and I continued to search, trying to figure out what was happening to me. At the time I was going through this, I didn't understand what I was functionally doing. I thought this was just life. I was unaware of what I was ascribing worth to and too blind to see what I was worshipping with my time and attention. I couldn't see what my identity was wrapped up in. And all of this was affecting the way I was leading myself.

Application

I have taken you on a bit of my journey and will continue to throughout the remainder of the book, but there is purpose to this. The process of understanding more of your identity is just that— a process.

Before you continue reading, record your childhood experiences and earliest memories in writing. Use an outline, or perhaps just write down as many memories as you can in no particular order or even sequentially. Regardless of what method works best for you, what's important is to do it. An ordered timeline of events will help you paint the clearest picture of how your life continued to build upon itself.

Next, think about people who impacted you the most. Write down both painful and joyful memories; both are equally important. Be completely honest with yourself as you write about struggles or even addictions, whether you admitted to them at the time or not. Also record what you ran to for safety and security during those struggles. Who or what were your safe places?

Next on your writing journey, consider how your family saw you, and how you saw your family. Perceptions we have of others and perceptions people have of us really do matter. Write down what was going on in your head at these times. Think about what your family's beliefs were versus your beliefs. Be honest with yourself in how those beliefs may have changed, and if they did, when they started to change and how that change affected your actions.

Recording these thoughts is the starting point of knowing who you are and why you are the way you are. The most significant changes in life typically happen because of community, which is in essence, the people around us. As you go through this process, you'll probably have one significant person, or perhaps a few people, that impacted you in a monumental way. The next chapter explores the significance of this type of impact.

Utilize the space below to write down your memories:

3

THE ENCOUNTER THAT CHANGED EVERYTHING

During my senior year of college, on a sunny afternoon, I was walking briskly to a lunch date with a girl with whom I had reconnected with from childhood; I was very into her. I was running late, and I knew her to be a bit demanding, so I didn't want to agitate her. I didn't mind the fact that she was demanding because of what I was getting out of it.

I was just about to turn into the university center where we were meeting when three young Caucasian men stepped out in front of me and asked if they could ask me a few questions. I really wanted to walk right past them, but at that point, I would have felt like I was being rude. Also, it seemed it would take just a minute or two, so I reluctantly stopped and agreed to the questioning.

One guy stepped forward and introduced himself and asked if I could answer some questions about God. I thought that would be easy enough since I was a Christian, and I figured I would be finished quickly. He asked me ten questions that I thought I knew the answers to pretty well, so I rattled off my answers like a practiced and heady Christian guy would. As I was answering, he never challenged my answers. He kept saying "okay." When he finished with his questions, he asked if I would care to know the answers to his questions—and he asked in such a way that made me extremely intrigued (almost beguiled) to know how any of my responses were off. His loving inquiry about whether I wanted to know what the Bible said about these answers was so full of compassion and connection. I was floored! I thought to myself, *Didn't I just answer these questions correctly? What do you mean do I want to know the answers?! Well, of course I'd like to know how I was wrong!*

As you can imagine, more than a couple of minutes had passed. I was officially late to my date, but in those moments, I somehow was not bothered by that. The man began to provide insightful and Biblical answers to the ten questions he had asked me in a way that I had never heard before. I was challenged to the core of what I thought I knew and what I functionally believed. At the end of the entire conversation, this guy, who I thought was another college student, perhaps a grad student, informed me he was the pastor of a new church plant in Houston and told me of a campus program they were having that evening where they were raffling off an iPad.

I was more captivated, moved, touched, seen, heard, convicted, and valued in those few minutes than I had ever been in my life. I also could not believe he was a pastor because he did not fit into any idea I had of what a pastor should look or act like—at least, not from what I was used to. In my upbringing, especially coming from mostly African American churches, pastors were much older, sometimes compassionate, but often a bit surly and rigorous, with a rigid adherence to traditions and customs; they were also a bit unapproachable unless they approached you first. So, this encounter changed my entire perspective of pastors.

After that encounter that I really tried to avoid, I headed to my lunch date and, as you can imagine, it did not go well. She was pretty upset, despite my explanation of why I was late. Strangely, I was unbothered by her response as my mind was more preoccupied with my recent encounter. Our relationship pretty much ended there, but I was completely unaffected by it. I was enamored with what was going inside of me, as if something dead had been awakened; and I was convinced it was the Lord giving me hope and helping me realize that the misplaced values in my relationships were not the extent of my identity.

I was looking forward to the evening when the campus program began. I couldn't wait to see what it was all about. Finally, 6:00 PM came, I walked in briskly, got my raffle ticket for the iPad, and walked past at least a hundred students as I made my way to sit on the very first row. I wanted to see and feel more of what I had encountered earlier that day with this pastor. We heard singing from an eclectic-looking group of young people full of passion, life and energy. Then, a guy got up to speak to students about God using apologetics. If you are unfamiliar with the word *apologetics*, please note that it does not mean the same thing as apologize, as in being sorry for something. *Apologetics* comes from the ancient Greek word *apologia*, which means "speaking in defense." So, apologetics is essentially defending doctrine through reasoned and systematic arguments.

After the minister was done speaking, I knew that I had to be a part of whatever this was. I was in a place of searching and felt such a void in my life that I kept trying to fill with what never quite satisfied or fulfilled me: I knew that relationships and accolades could not do it; I also knew that I had found no other sort of social "high" that could do it. My identity went only as far as those things could take me, so I was unstable, insecure, unsure of myself, and even aimless at that point. But that day, something changed: I felt a sense of hope I had never known before.

This moment, in October of 2010, was a pivotal encounter that placed me on a trajectory in life I could not have foreseen. In life, I have come to realize that we can both make moments in life and make the most out of them; but sometimes, moments in life can make the most out of us. This was definitely a time where the moment made the most out of me.

Application

Encounters or experiences like this can either significantly build on our current frame or may in fact build a completely new frame. At the time, we may not realize it because we are always in the "here and now." Even while reading this book and after having written down your memories, a moment like this may seem minimally significant or even insignificant. However, years from this very moment, you could look back with a much different perspective and see an impact you cannot perceive presently. The same can be said of our encounters each and every day. Some encounters, even in those here-and-now moments, are pivotal and can be easily spotted as such. Then there are those encounters that seem small, but create a ripple effect all throughout the course of our lives that we cannot perceive at the time. These are frame-building and frame-making moments.

Our frames say a lot about us. When you think about the frame of a structure, you have an idea of what it can support and a bit about how the structure will look once complete. Your frame is the building block of the rest of discovering your identity. Your frame even determines what you take in as significant. It determines what you interpret as a value-add moment, a value-add person, idea, or principle. You filter everything through how you are framed.

The following chapter takes you through discovering your identity and building on your frame.

4

AN ADVENTURE TOWARD DISCOVERING IDENTITY

In the fall of 2010, during my senior year of college, I made up my mind that I was done with women and relationships. I knew I couldn't handle that along with trying to figure out who I was. Don't get me wrong; I liked women, but I determined that I would not intentionally seek out a relationship. I had made up my mind that it was something I was neither ready for nor wanted any longer. With one failed relationship after another in the past, I thought, *What's the point? I'm just going to be single for the rest of my life, and I think I will be okay with that.*

At the same time I made up my mind to enter the world of eternal singledom, I began attending the church that the pastor I met on my college campus had planted. It was a new church plant, so not very many people attended; but it was full of love and people with big hearts. The worship, the music, the way church was done was so dynamically different from what I was used to. I felt comfortable and at home there. I was not being preached at but rather brought into the conversation of Christianity much differently than I had experienced in previous churches I had attended. It seemed more my speed—more me, in a sense. What I mean by that is that I am an analytical person—rational, methodical, logical, and very much a thinker and processor. When making decisions, I typically consider many angles, process internally and mentally, weigh the options and courses of actions, and consider the ramifications. After taking in as much information, research, and proven and tested available resources as I can find, I then finally make the best decision I can based on what I have learned. I'm hardwired that way. The dialogue that was happening with me personally at this church, with the pastor, and from the messages, all appealed to me in this way. I was able to process and realize things through my internal hardwiring system, and the messages were delivered in a way that lent itself to be considered and processed through this practical approach.

In my first week attending this church, the pastor preached from a book of the Bible called Song of Solomon. I had never in my life heard a sermon preached from that particular book of the

Bible. It rocked me to my core because this book was like a blueprint left by God on how to create healthy and meaningful relationships from courtship to engagement, to marriage, and then navigating marriage. I was left speechless. I realized how terrible I had been at relationships— not because they had all failed, but because I began to realize *why* they had failed. I was shown how I viewed women, and more importantly, how that view came from a sense of how I viewed myself. I was dealing with the women I dated based on my own identity, which was faulty at best. I saw that I couldn't possibly have a healthy relationship with another human being when the most important relationship, the one with myself, was unrealized, misunderstood, rooted in lies I believed about myself, and therefore others, and thus not healthy. I was leading with a demented and flawed view and perspective of who I was. To expect anything different by continuing to do the same thing without checking myself first is quite literally insane.

As I mentioned before, this realization occurred through the way I am hardwired. At the time, I did not even recognize the way I was hardwired and how I processed information. It was not something I thought about or considered, but as I came to understand more about myself, this became more and more clear to me and allowed me to navigate this relational issue head on. The way this message was presented to me, from the Song of Solomon, was through the exact way I came to realizations to make decisions—through my hardwiring of processing, analyzing, etc. This particular message that I heard, and the way in which it was presented, kick-started a lot of self-realization and became the starting point of even how I came to write this book.

I had never heard anything preached from the Bible through practical terms, through logical terms, through terms that directly related to me and appealed to me through the very way I processed information. It was not until that moment that it started to dawn on me just how I processed information and why this particular message was so convicting, convincing, and relevant to my current situation and state of mind. It was a true turning point in my life, which is why I am spending a great deal of time on this issue. It cannot be overlooked, so please consider not just what I am writing, but the application of what I am writing.

The message that came through to me from Song of Solomon connected to me through the way I was hardwired and allowed me to navigate through thoughts and ideas in the Bible in a manner I had never experienced. Though not every message was delivered through the exact way I processed, I was able to take each one through my process and see how it all came together. Before, Biblical messages were presented to me in such a way that I was not able to do that—the presentation seemed out of reach, so I failed to connect to it and weigh it.

Application

It is imperative to evaluate how you process and make decisions. Without a more complete sense of how you are hardwired, you may remain aimless, neglect yourself and others, compromise your integrity, and even waste resources in the wrong areas. Having a better sense of your hardwiring should also humble you. Once you realize in a more complete way a certain aspect of yourself, you should know this is not true of everyone else, and other's people's positions and thought processes should be just as valued as your own. I am not saying everyone is true or always right, but I am saying you are able to better value people, and not neglect or dismiss their process and their thoughts. It enables you to appeal to people based on their hardwiring.

The Search for Identity Continues

As is the case with many people in their early twenties, I struggled to find what I was meant to do in life and what it was that I was truly passionate about. I knew it had something to do with helping people but was not quite sure how I was going to spend the rest of my life doing it.

Much of this I internalized as being a failure. I felt an enormous amount of pressure to have come to a decision about what I was supposed to be aiming towards. But I knew I had to aim somewhere that was at least somewhat appealing. My mind was so preoccupied with how I would make a living, pondering whether I would make enough to live decently or be able to support a family if that happened someday, if I was smart enough for anything. I wasn't solidly sure of anything, and I was still trying to figure out the person I wanted to be. My identity was taking a beating in many areas that mattered, but not in all of them.

As I began to understand how I processed information, how I looked at women and dealt with relationships, it brought me back full circle to look more intently at myself and everything with which I was truly struggling. This internal struggle was like a firmly entrenched root that was impacting my effectiveness at leading myself, leading in the way of relationships, and leadership ability with work later on in life.

I started attending my new church in the fall of 2010 and joined soon thereafter. Though the message from the Song of Solomon was a pivotal message for me, I needed to discern and address other issues. As I mentioned, I was a senior in college at that time, and I struggled to find what I was truly passionate about, and what I was meant to do in life.

My initial goal was to be either an optometrist or an ophthalmologist, but I was not hugely passionate about either. I knew I wanted to make a difference somehow, and I knew I would need to find a job after college. I struggled in many areas of college life—discipline to study, academics, and staying focused.

In my last month of college in 2010, I landed my first job with the local Lions Eye Bank of Texas. That is not what it sounds like. It is not any kind of financial institution. It is an establishment in the health care setting that is primarily responsible for the retrieval of ocular tissue from decedents for the purpose of transplanting to help bring the gift of sight restoration. I thought this job would be a springboard perhaps into a career as a future optometrist or ophthalmologist. Though the prospect of being a doctor didn't appeal to me still, it seemed to be an available option to provide for myself, and I knew it would make my family proud to have a doctor in the family. And I did not know of any other career track with a biology education that would enable me to make a decent living.

All of that notwithstanding, I was truly excited with my first job as an eye recovery technician working at the Lions Eye Bank. It was new, exciting, and something so radically different than any other job. It was always a fun conversation, for me at least, when someone asked me what I did for work.

Meeting Dad's Expectations

I knew my dad would be extremely proud if I became a doctor. It was a topic that he visited a lot as I was growing up. The idea of his son becoming a doctor seemed to be the icing on the cake for him. If I voiced anything less, it did not seem to go over too well. In this time in my life, I definitely felt like I had the golden child syndrome, and it weighed on me heavily. If you are unfamiliar with the term "golden child syndrome," it is when a child suffers from the immense burden of expectation placed on their shoulders by family or loved ones, but especially and significantly by their parents.

I also had the self-induced stress of performance, striving for a successful life, and living out the rest of my life as perfectly as possible. I had set an impossible task for myself, one that I could never live up to and needed to be free of. However, I had no idea where to start. So, I continued trying to meet these impossible expectations which, in some ways, caused me to push harder in areas of life when I otherwise probably would not have. I was living and working ultimately for the approval and satisfaction of my dad and also the rest of my family. I felt that when I met that, then I could marinate a bit in the satisfaction and success of that accomplishment.

This foundational part of my identity growing up was unintentionally reinforced time and time again. No intentional mandate was placed on me to perform and live for the satisfaction and approval of my father and family, but this is how I interpreted my upbringing in a lot of ways. Let me just say that my father was and is an amazing father. He loved me fiercely and sacrificed astronomically to help raise me along with my mother, support me, and push me as a loving father would. What father does not want to see his son succeed in life? I did not grow up questioning the love my father or the rest of my family had for me. I grew up questioning the love I had for myself and what I wanted to do with my life. I did not even begin to face that crossroad in life until my last year of college; and even then, it was years later before I truly realized where my passions lay and where they would take me and stopped living for the approval of others.

Relate and Understand

I tell you this because my story is likely relatable to many of you. Most of us grow up with a guardian to guide us, lead us, raise us, and show us the way so-to-speak. They are working from a place of their life experiences, upbringing, expectations, and where they are currently in life as they rear another human being. As we grow up under this umbrella and their methodology of teaching, grooming, and approach to life, we are expected to behave a certain way, live a certain way, and make certain kinds of approved decisions. So, we are all, to some extent, conditioned by and products of our upbringing. It's nature and nurture working together.

We all should, however, reach a point in life where we begin thinking more independently, looking more inwardly, and asking questions we probably dared never ask before. Our identities are shaped from the moment we take our first breath in this life, because those identities are first fashioned and formed by those raising us. Those raising us have the first significant imprint on our identity makeup. This begins to shape our frame, cognition, self-awareness, awareness of others, and, in effect, how we would interact with people and lead them. More importantly, identity is a starting point in defining how you will lead yourself. The person you are today is not and never has been completely shaped and determined by just you. It's been significantly shaped by others—first and foremost, by those who had a hand in raising you. Ask yourself at this point, *What am I living for? How am I leading, and who am I leading? What do I place value in?* We will explore this more in depth later in the book, but these are significant starting points in realizing where you are, who you are, and asking questions of yourself, and perhaps even others, that you never thought or even dared to ask before. Understand, the answers to these questions will not remain stagnant throughout your life. All three answers will change either a little or a lot and may even change by the time you finish this book.

Take time to think about the answers to those questions as you understand them to be now, and jot them down in the space provided below:

What or who am I living for?

_____

_____

_____

_____

_____

_____

How am I leading, and who am I leading?

_____

_____

_____

_____

_____

_____

What do I place value in?

_____

_____

_____

_____

_____

_____

Encounter with Alethea

With college behind me and a new job ahead, I was looking for something new and fresh; I felt I was in a place of aimless stagnation and unprepared for what was occurring. Attending a new church came with providential timing since the church was only a few months old.

Having been hugely convicted by the series of messages from the Song of Solomon, I realized that I had gone about relationships in a very unhealthy way. As I said, heading into 2011, I made up my mind to stop pursuing relationships with women and resolved that I would be okay if I were single for the rest of my life. I was changing my mentality and needed time to reflect and process life in a healthy manner in this area and others that were so broken, perverted, and demented. It was like a reset for me and a fresh new start with a completely different set of worldview lenses.

From the time I was thirteen, I played piano in church for praise and worship. I am completely self-taught and play by ear, which means I can play what I hear. In my new church, I determined not to play anymore. I just wanted to sit and consume. I did not expect to give, contribute, or serve because I thought it was all about me. I thought I was supposed to simply receive and hear what I needed to hear in order to reset so many areas of my life. Boy, was I wrong!

In early 2011, I attended a membership class hosted by the pastor and his wife at their house because our meeting space inside a rented-out theater room was available only on Sundays. In that class, I noticed a pretty young woman, but my first thought was that she had beautiful eyes. (I worked at an eye bank, remember, so eyes were usually the first thing I noticed about someone new.) I was not looking to become romantically involved with anyone, so I did not pay her any attention after our introduction, but I was smitten by her name. She introduced herself as Alethea (Uh-lee-thee-uh). I remember thinking, *Wow, what a beautiful name!* before introducing myself and thinking that "Emmitt" just did not have the same cool ring to it as "Alethea."

After an inspirational membership meeting, the pastor asked if I would consider playing piano with the worship team. I was floored. Right off the bat, I had two opportunities staring me in the face that I had already determined I would not pursue: women and playing the piano. It was easy to say no to pursuing Alethea, whom I had just met; but it was a different story regarding the request to use my gift of music to serve in the church. Somehow, this felt different...like a reset as opposed to just doing the same ol' thing. I pondered his request for what seemed like several minutes but, in reality, was only a few seconds. I wanted to refuse, but somehow reluctantly agreed. It was unknowingly the best "yes" I could have said, because it set me on a trajectory that led to so many great life victories and also to the writing of this book ten years later.

I began playing with the worship team right away, and guess who was singing on that team? You guessed it—Alethea from membership class. She was usually a background singer, but when I heard her do mic checks, I thought she sounded like an angel. Her voice was soft, yet so full of love, grace, calmness, and stillness. Still, my thoughts about her went no further than that.

During this time, my life seemed a bit more peaceful. I was still discovering more fully and deeply who I was, who I wanted to become, and what I wanted to do. I found more satisfaction in my work as an eye recovery technician working at the eye bank, began to excel there, and became very skilled at the job. Other things in life that seemed to weigh me down began gradually falling off of me. I was feeling freer and less burdened with life's worries, even though I was not completely rid of them. It was a process for sure.

Application

This time period in my life is analogous to a sculptor making small nicks and chiseling away at seemingly insignificant pieces of his creation. However, the collective efforts of each small change began to reveal something rather exquisite. This is what was happening to me, though I didn't see it during those moments of being chiseled and refined.

The refining process happens to all of us, as we will see if we pause to reflect on those moments. Each time we move closer to a place of better understanding or even sometimes confusion, experience moments of peace as well as turmoil, experience an overwhelming sense of satisfaction as well as dissatisfaction, it is imperative that we not ignore those moments. The fact that we remember and count moments, experiences, and encounters as significant, and the fact that they produce a combustion of emotions or a flood of thoughts, ideas, goals, visions, or dreams that may or may not lead to a response or reaction, is the reason these experiences are to be counted as part of our identity development. It shows us what we value. In chapter seven, we'll take a deeper dive into values and how they play out in our lives and identities as well as our effectiveness as leaders.

5

EXPECTATIONS

When I met Alethea, I was not looking for a relationship, mainly because I knew I needed to change because my relationships were all ending the same way. The sermons from the Song of Solomon helped me realize my faulty perspective and view of women and relationships, and I repented of my folly. I realized the damage I had done to myself as well as to those with whom I had been in relationship. I was sorrowful, yet, for the first time, felt a weight lifted off my shoulders; I felt free of tainted thinking and understanding and was able to lead myself in a healthy way to make different decisions and even behave differently.

Meeting Expectations as A Husband

Once this tainted lens fell from my eyes, Alethea did not look quite the same to me. For the sake of brevity, I won't go into every detail because that would be pages upon pages of everything I began to see and feel about her. I will say this. Since my worldview of women and relationships was turned upside down, the way in which I saw this woman, the way in which she appealed to me, was radically different from any woman in the past. For the first time, I beheld her beauty from the inside rather than the outside. The reverse had always been true; I had typically given very little weight to inner beauty.

After several months, I mustered up the courage to ask Alethea out, and we started dating in May of 2011. I proposed to her in February of 2012, and we married in October of 2012.

Marriage was, of course, a major life milestone. Life changes significantly. We did our best to prepare properly for marriage by going through pre-marital counseling and making a mutual decision as we were dating that we would not put ourselves in compromising situations. So, we didn't kiss on the lips, have sex, or spend the night over at each other's place. We did not want to awaken that part our relationship until we married, and I could not be any more glad or joyful today about that mutual decision.

Some of you may be thinking we're crazy, that we should have "played house" while we dated. While I'm aware that much of our society thinks that way, I was convicted and convinced that we were not to do it that way. In fact, many studies reveal a correlation between divorce rates in couples and pre-marital cohabitation. The Institute for Family Studies reports: "There remains an increased risk for divorce for those living together prior to marriage, and that prior studies suggesting the effect has gone away had a bias toward short versus longer-term effects. They find that living together before marriage is associated with lower odds of divorce in the first year of marriage but increases the odds of divorce in all other years tested, and this finding holds across decades of data."

Our decision to go about our relationship the way we did was based on mandates of God's Word, and I am using this example to help you understand a bit more context regarding who I am and how our shaped identities influence and impact our leadership.

In this new stage of life as a husband, I encountered new expectations to lead my wife in ways and areas that had never been of any concern to me. Marriage is looked at and treated so differently depending on one's upbringing, culture, religion, and even irreligion. To me, as a Christian, marriage is a binding, lifelong, and unconditional covenant made not only to the person I am marrying, but to God before a witness of people that can hold me accountable. I really could spend the rest of this book going into all of that, but for brevity's sake, I'll say that marriage was no small act, as I understood it to be a commitment like no other that required me to be a man of integrity, honesty, truth, conviction, strength, wisdom, love, joy, peace, patience, gentleness, kindness and self-control. I had to learn *how* to lead my wife, as well as myself, in those areas. And that all looks different on a practical level for each couple as they spend a lifetime learning more and more about each other every day. Marriage is an endless sea of discovery.

On a practical level, as someone who is introverted and an internal processor who had, up to that point, spent my entire life wrapped up in silently processing and thinking in my head, I never thought about articulating my thoughts out loud and bringing someone else into that space and journey of my thought process. For over two decades, the only person I ever had to communicate with was myself. In marriage, suddenly with a flip of the switch, that all *had to* change; and I did not realize right away that it must change, nor did I know exactly how to change. Marriage is a most helpful mirror as it allows you to see yourself from a new perspective—the perspective of your spouse. Effective communication is a must, not only in marriage, but in any relationship. I will forever remember this quote from our pastor and his wife: "Communication is the foundation of every relationship."

I have held this truth near and dear to my heart since hearing it more than eleven years ago now. A significant expectation that I initially, yet unintentionally, overlooked was bringing Alethea into my head space. Men are not typically very good at expressing our thoughts and emotions, especially to women. We communicate and process life differently than they do. Men, in general, are linear and compartmentalized thinkers and processors without much emotion attached to it. Women, in general, think and process with emotion attached to it, and everything is related and intertwined. Neither way is better than the other, but it is important to understand the difference and how it affects your partner's thinking.

However, as a husband, I had to be intentional and do things differently as I was made more aware of when I was not communicating well so that I could lead in love, kindness, and wisdom. When I was not bringing my wife into my process, I unknowingly communicated rejection, unkindness, and even foolishness toward her, the very opposite of what and how I should be leading and communicating.

I was one to want to quickly get a problem fixed, find the resolution, be the perfect husband, and do no wrong. So, I expected of myself that I wouldn't create problems, but that I would avoid them at all costs; and I expected my wife to do the same. This was an internal desire and expectation I placed on both of us, but more so on myself. I wanted our marriage to be problem-free and perfect.

When that didn't happen, I felt more and more defeated. When I hurt my wife emotionally by excluding her from my thoughts, I felt like I had failed her; but I unknowingly internalized this so deeply that I not only felt like a failure but identified as a failure. I began thinking that I was a terrible husband and leader. My identity began to take on this belief. It was a huge blow to my confidence because this was one area where I had stood up before so many and vowed to God and my wife that I would love and lead her, a responsibility I willingly accepted; but I was spinning my wheels trying to figure out where I was going wrong. Unbeknownst to me, I was spinning my wheels in the wrong direction.

Application

Milestones such as marriage are forever life changing. Such a milestone can reveal much about who you are and what you are made of. It reveals even our selfish ambitions and motives. New expectations are placed upon us that, in my opinion, make us better and deepen and broaden our understanding of ourselves and those with whom we are in community.

Unchecked expectations, especially for those in a marriage or in a romantic relationship of any sort, will lead to instability in that relationship and instability within yourself. A relationship such as marriage is to be treated tenderly, like a garden or a vineyard. It requires care and attention and preventative action to ensure the health, growth, and stability of the garden. I often remember and reflect on this verse from Song of Solomon 2:15 in Scripture: *"Catch the foxes for us, the little foxes that are ruining the vineyards, while our vineyards are in blossom"* (NASB2020). The woman of the relationship is speaking to her lover, asking him to do what is needed to protect their love relationship from problems that could harm it. The foxes referred to in the verse represent those problems and issues, unmet expectations even, that—if unchecked and not dealt with—will, like a fox trampling and ruining a vineyard, be detrimental to the relationship.

You might be wondering what all of this has to do with identity. It has much to do with it. When you are in any season of life, embarking upon a significant change that requires a great deal of investment and commitment, such as a committed relationship, naturally becomes a reflection of who you are based on actions you repeatedly have to take every day, and thus it feeds into your identity. Those looking at this garden or vineyard so to speak, which is your marriage or a relationship, will perceive what is projected. What they perceive of that, and more importantly, what you perceive of it, spotlights in more ways than one the kind of person you are and the new identity you have taken on and now take in.

Meeting Expectations as a Coworker

Another area of life worth delving into, as anyone above working age in America can relate to, is our jobs.

I experienced many changes in life all around the same exact time. It was both exciting and scary. I acquired both a new bride and a new job in the same month, two new roles and responsibilities that I needed to continue learning and becoming better at.

My role at my new job was very different than any other job I had before. It was very team-based, although it included work I performed independently of the team. Being an introvert, an analytical internal processor and thinker, I was forced to go a bit beyond my default style of operating. I was the youngest full-time employee in my department, as well as the least experienced. And because of this, I felt underqualified for the position and intimidated by just about everybody. I often had feelings of excitement and eagerness mixed with nervousness and anxiety to perform well. I knew

I was expected to learn quickly and do the work without a monumental mistake or failure. This role required great attention to detail, critical thinking skills, effective and proficient communication, and an enormous amount of adaptability.

I struggled a bit in my humble beginnings, and every move I made was looked at like I was under a microscope—from coworkers more than management. These were the people I had to work beside every single day, so I had to figure out how to shape up, adapt, and learn as quickly as I could. I did not want to let my teammates down and did want to do everything I could to serve and work as diligently as possible. The training was intense at times. The hours were both long and intense as I worked an on-call schedule—something I had to get used to. I was expected to quickly adapt to both the cognitive and physical requirements of this new role.

All the while, I was trying to balance work, home life and my responsibilities within the church. I was carrying quite a load with high expectations on every front. Being the kind of person that I am, I was determined to do it all perfectly, flawlessly, and without burnout. I added to those expectations by placing a self-expectation of perfection that may have been a tad bit ambitious but was honestly unrealistic.

Still, I resolved to work hard and do everything I could with excellence, trying each and every day to never make the same mistake twice—and, in reality, I was trying not to make a mistake at all. I remember one of my trainers saying to me when I first started, "Who knows? Perhaps one day, you'll be the one teaching me something." He made me realize I could do this job and do it well. He may not have meant what he said to be encouraging, but it was profoundly encouraging to me. I internalized his words, and they ignited within me a hunger and passion for my work. I became determined to be the best (competition), to help others be their best (inclusion), and to take responsibility for every task I had been assigned to perform (responsibility).

My number one strength, according to the StrengthsFinder assessment I took, is *responsibility.* Number two is *includer,* and number three is *competition.* Over thirty other strengths are placed in an order of dominance that's unique to everyone, but for the sake of brevity and sticking to the point, I have listed only my top three. These are themes that I operate in by default. For example, my strength of responsibility means that I take psychological ownership of what I say I will do and am committed to stable values such as honesty and loyalty. However great that may sound, it is profoundly difficult to push myself to say no, so I found myself being agreeable to almost everything asked of me. My capacity to own all of that often kept me from sharing responsibility, as I had a difficult time even beginning to understand how I would do that.

My dominant strengths add to not only the expectations from coworkers and management, but the expectations I place on myself in the roles I undertake. My strengths serve me well in the area of meeting expectations, but they can just as equally serve to cloud my judgment and perception of who I am, what I can and cannot do, what I should and should not do, and how I treat others around me.

Application

Some of you may relate to this all too well, and some of you may think I'm nuts, asking yourselves, "Why in the world would anyone want more and more responsibility?" A bit of that answer is due to nature and a bit of it is due to nurture, so both internal and external factors make up how and why we are the way we are. However, regardless of our default themes or strengths, if unchecked by the right people, these themes or strengths can also cripple us if we are not careful. If you have never taken a personality assessment, I would encourage you to do so; it will be helpful in gaining a better understanding of yourself as well as hopefully providing insight into the kinds of people you can partner with that complement you and help you in your blind spots. Unfortunately, I did not give much weight to being helped in my blind spots. I focused solely on what I was good at until it began to get the better of me.

Jobs, for many people, are their identity. We often ask people when we first meet them, "So, what do you do?" How many times have you been asked that, and how many times have you asked a new acquaintance that question in social settings? Even in corporate meetings, it is commonplace to identity people by their role, title, and thus relevancy to any particular meeting or project, or the question is used as an icebreaker. As we do this over and over, especially at work, we continually reinforce our relevancy and thus our identity through our titles, positions, and expected roles we are there to carry out.

The purpose of taking a personality assessment is not to help you understand your relevancy to your work, group, or project. Identity is about understanding yourself and bringing more awareness of what makes you, well, *you.*

Fatherhood and Developing a False Sense of Self Due to Lies I Believed

A couple of months after we married, my wife and I discovered we were going to have a baby. I remember when she first told me the news, I could see a bit of worry in her face. I had but seconds to respond. I felt an immediate flood of emotions and thoughts I had to quickly process as I knew our lives were about to change for the rest of our lives. Though this was not what we had planned for our first couple of years of marriage, here we were. As I saw my wife's facial expression as she waited for my response, I could see that she was understandably overcome with worry. However, as I collected my explosion of thoughts and emotions, I smiled and expressed my excitement. I refused to allow fear to rule. We just couldn't. We had a life coming into the world for whom we would be responsible. Though we did not have the first clue about being parents, nor were we even lightly seasoned in our marriage, the only step we could take was forward. I was truly excited about being a dad.

However, excitement soon faded as I began recalling what was said about me before Alethea and I married and comments people close to Alethea made to her regarding me. Though we had addressed those things and dismissed and pummeled them, they came flooding back into my head and began to plant seeds of doubt, discouragement, and lies I began to believe and function out of. Unwisely, I did not initially discuss any of this with my wife. I was determined to process it and deal with it internally due to my default manner of dealing with life. I am an internal processor and analyzer.

The lies I believed were that I was not God's best for Alethea, that I was a deceiver, and that our marriage would fail because I was not the person Alethea thought me to be. The sad thing is that only two people, who will remain nameless, made these assertions. Out of the hundreds of people, close friends, and family we know and love, only *two* people's words wrought havoc in my mind and became lies I believed so strongly that I internalized them and functionally identified as a failure. And the even sadder part is that, at the time, these two people really did not know me at all. However, I took what they said to heart. I did not believe that I would make a great dad, nor did I believe I was being a great husband. I battled this alone every waking moment of each day.

Thoughts and Actions

Psychologically speaking, our brains are more highly sensitive to unpleasant and negative news because our brains have what is called a "negativity bias." Dr. John Cacioppa showed that the brain reacts more strongly to stimuli it deems negative and has a greater surge in electrical activity. Thus, our attitudes are more heavily influenced by negative news than good news.[1]

This comes as no surprise. We tend to fixate on the negatives, the problems, and especially what we perceive as danger. Relationships can suffer greatly if we're not combating our negative thoughts and false beliefs about ourselves with encouraging and positive ones. When we do not do this, those negatives begin to permeate our lives and relationships, even the relationship with ourselves, and thus we behave from a newly and negatively formed state of being.

Meeting Expectations as a Father

When bringing a child into the world, a parent is overcome with all sorts of thoughts. A common thought or desire is *wanting* to be a great parent. My wife and I were determined to do the best we possibly could at this parenting thing. We began reading books and articles, listening to podcasts, reflecting on how we were parented, and communicating regarding what we would and would not emulate, and how we would and would not discipline.

I believe it right to say that, as parents, we tend to place an expectation on ourselves to have our parenting look a certain way. We also place expectations on the other parent or significant

---

[1] *Our Brain's Negative Bias.* Estroff, Hara. Published June 20, 2003. Psychology Today.

other who is helping raise the child, but we will all fall short of some of those ideals.

As a new dad, I learned a lot about myself and my capacities. I was refined in many ways as my patience was tested. I experienced a plethora of both unpleasantries and pleasantries that facilitated growth and development as a parent.

Any parent must learn to create margin and build healthy balances between work and home. If not, danger is lurking around the corner. I worked a lot and was no stranger to long hours. I was trying to provide for my family as we were a single-income family. My wife and I thought it best for her to be a full-time stay-at-home mom, and thankfully were able to make that happen. I know that's not for everyone, but it was and still is the case for us. Being that I worked a lot, I felt like I missed out on a lot; after the first year and half of my son's life, I suddenly came to the realization that I made more of a priority out of work than my family. My son was developing abilities that I did not realize he had, and I found myself suddenly in a state of amazement and bewilderment at how much he had grown. I had missed out on the process, and it hurt me deeply. I had deprived my son of his father in the first almost two years of his life, and I had deprived my wife of showing her a more loving and present father and husband.

My wife was so full of grace and love as I brought up this sudden awareness I had of the situation and explained that I needed to and had to do better. I began with making and communicating a clear schedule of work and family time and attempted to create boundaries between the two. This was golden, and I found myself better able to enjoy life and able to be more fully present, not just physically, but with intentional attention and energy.

At this two-year mark of being a parent, I had just received a promotion at work; my wife and I were thrilled about the new opportunity. However, with the promotion came new responsibilities as well as immense challenges. At church, not too long before my promotion at work, I had been asked to be the music director and thus lead the band and other musical elements during Sunday morning worship. Here I was serving in two very different places, suddenly plunged into new leadership positions with a responsibility to people I was expected to lead. The other similarity between these two roles was that I was being promoted from within—from frontline to a leadership role, serving and leading the line that I came from. Did I feel ready? Not quite. Did I feel like I knew exactly what I was doing? Not entirely.

As I began this journey in these leadership roles, my passion for leadership grew exponentially. Perspectives changed. I was not one to attempt to usurp authority. On one hand, as I held the responsibility of being a music director, I understood it to be more than just leading the band and having a plan musically for Sunday morning worship; I was serving the needs of the team and the congregation and shepherding souls. On the other hand, at my place of work, I was also serving the needs of the team and ultimately the community our organization serves. The challenge in this, though, came when my colleagues looked at me as this young guy who was just on the frontlines serving with them who had suddenly been given a bit more authority and responsibility to lead them. I was not looked at as someone with an enormous amount of expertise and experience, so respect was not just automatically handed to me by all; the change involved a struggle and many hard lessons learned to earn that respect. However, the point is that, with the new positions at both work and church, I had new roles and responsibilities to try and balance out with my renewed commitment to my home life.

I was pulled in multiple directions and, being the person I am with a high-functioning responsibility theme, I wanted to do it all so perfectly. I intensely care for the well-being of those around me, regardless of where I am positionally, and that is especially true of my family. Who I am began to be wrapped up in how well I did, based on my own expectations as well as those of others, in these significant areas of my life: leading my family, leading the band at church, and leading my colleagues at work. So, I rested in approval of and satisfaction with myself to the degree to which I did those things well in my own eyes as well as in the eyes of others. My identity became directly linked to my approval ratings in each of those area.

Application

The evaluated experience here teaches that it is normal for us to place expectations on ourselves, and we will always have expectations placed on us by others, especially those close to us, those with whom we work, and those we have a responsibility to lead. The question becomes, what happens to our view of self when those expectations we impose on ourselves or that others place on us—whether positive or negative—are not met? This helps us to understand what we are defined by as we delve into what our reactions or responses to that would be. The next chapter delves into that a bit and, from a bit of my story, you'll see some of the impacts these challenges had on me and how these realizations can be applied for you. I experienced many problems that can be avoided by simply recognizing the pitfalls long before you get to them.

6

THE FALL

The promotions at both my job and church took a lot of work, energy, and time. I was working forty to fifty hours a week, and sometimes more. My church responsibilities required ten to twenty hours a week. In total, a work week for me ranged from fifty to seventy hours a week. While that may be an average amount of time for some, especially entrepreneurs, that is well above average for people with families.

My full-time job is what mostly affected me. I found work becoming increasingly stressful, mostly due to having fallen short of meeting the expectations of both staff and myself. I had much to learn, and I needed to learn it quickly. I worked long hours—anywhere from twelve to twenty-four hours straight. I was expected to train people at work, create and implement a high-quality training program and curriculum from scratch, while also meeting the staff's expectation of being available at all times to solve the woes of the team. And whenever I couldn't fill a hole or provide support in every possible way on any given day or in any given week, it seemed I lost respect and a bit of influence. It was hard to accomplish tasks because I did not have the ear of the staff. It was extremely frustrating. So, because I felt I needed to work more, I did. I tried to be present as much as I could, and when I was not, I felt like I failed. Whenever I saw trust and respect fading from staff, I felt that I had failed. My continued striving inevitably took time from my family as I was less present at home. When I realized how that affected my family, I felt like a failure there as well. I began to view myself as a failure in two significant areas of my life.

I was spiraling down, but I kept trying to fix it by using the same approach—work more hours and be more present at home. While temporary changes seemed to help in one area, which provided a sense of accomplishment for me, this inevitably took away success from the other area; and I found myself right back in the same spot. It was as if I was playing whack-a-mole on all fronts, but I had not yet realized the changes I needed to make.

For several years, I tried desperately to hold myself together and perform all of my responsibilities well, like the responsible person I was. However, inwardly, I did not have it all together. My soul was in turmoil, and I was under tremendous stress. My blood pressure was consistently through the roof, attributed to how poorly I was managing work and home. I needed a release button and an escape.

I began turning to anything that would distract me from reality. For men, that can manifest in many different ways. I am not here to judge people on what they turn to, but simply to point out that whatever it is, it detaches us from those around us—often with negative consequences. I basically turned into a turtle; I bottled up my thoughts and feelings and shut out my wife and loved ones from the reality of what I was dealing with. I scrolled social media as often as I could and made work my mistress because instant gratification was more easily accomplished there than in the other areas of my life. I knew my industry, I was growing and excelling and receiving kudos for my work, so I focused on work more intensely than anything else. I resolved to figure out everything else on my own, but that approach just caused me to grow distant from my wife.

As time went on and the pressure slowly built, what I could not escape was my own feelings of failure. I was not dealing with my life in a healthy manner, and deep down I knew it. But I also did not know what the answer would be other than to keep doing the only thing I knew to do—try harder on all fronts. This had devastating effects on my mental well-being. My thoughts became increasingly suicidal. I thought of it as the ultimate escape and how I would manage to rid the world of a failure and therefore free everyone from my shortcomings and their frustrations. I pondered ways to kill myself without causing pain. I also wondered if I would receive God's forgiveness and make it into heaven if I committed suicide. I was even trying to plot an escape plan for my escape plan.

An opportunity presented itself on a work trip at the peak of this desperate season in my life. Neither my wife nor I were sure if I'd return home in a body bag or just return home. While alone in my hotel room on this trip, I thought to myself, "This is it!" I was going to end my life. Just then, I began to pray, "Lord, please..." but I never finished that prayer, because as I got to the word *please,* I saw a picture in my head of my wife and children mourning the loss of a husband and father. No one was celebrating my life or legacy. They were, in fact, in a worse state of mind in my vision than they were in presently. That would have been what I left behind. Right then and there, I snapped out of my defeated mindset and asked God for forgiveness. I had reached the end of myself and was on the edge...I firmly believe that God brought me back from the brink of suicide.

Application

We are not immune to allowing stressors of life to take over. Isolated stressors add up, if allowed, and amount to something that seems overwhelmingly difficult to deal with and thus causes distortion of our focus and our view of our self-image. We begin identifying and defining ourselves not by our successes, but by our failures and unpleasantries in life. Our natural tendency is to fix or remove what seems unpleasant. When stressors cloud the lens through which we see our individual world where we have direct influence or by which we are directly influenced, out of desperation and hopelessness, we can fall prey to the rock-bottom belief that the best way to fix it is to free ourselves from that world. This last act, quite literally, is in fact the worst way to fix the problem.

We each have a purpose, and we each have a story. Some may not believe in a higher purpose for human life on earth. I do, and that is what gives me hope. Without that belief, I would see this life as a useless and purposeless void. Each of us has entered in this world in just the exact time and place we are supposed to occupy.

Problems do not fix themselves if we ignore them. We can change certain things about ourselves that influence and shape the world around us. When that begins to happen, that's our identity at work. Continue reading to see how the story of identity, and even your story, is practically walked out.

7

THE RISE

I had reached the end of myself, but fortunately did not go through with suicide. I had come to my senses and realized how selfish that choice would have been, and it certainly was in no way the answer I was seeking.

I first recognized that I needed to open up to my wife. How I was dealing with my problems and processing was one-sided, closed off, and in some ways a functional rejection of her and those who loved me and wanted what was best for me. I remember first starting to be vulnerable with her in a way that I never had, and it was one of the sweetest moments my wife and I have ever experienced. It was the first time in a very long time that I felt hope and reassurance.

Around this same time, seemingly out of nowhere, some friends of ours sponsored us to attend a marriage retreat called *JH Outback*. They had no idea what was going on with us, but the timing could not have been better. This was a pivotal moment toward rediscovering who I was and certainly a significant boost in my marriage as we became more intentional with cultivating trust, openness, and honesty with one another.

Just a short time after the marriage retreat, we were again sponsored by another friend and our church to go through a week-long ministry of inner healing called *Restoring the Foundations*. This was a critical time for both of us of being reassured of who we were. So much was broken and bent inside of us that we did not recognize as being damaged. I was taken on a journey through the timeline of life, from my earliest memories to the present, to uproot and deal with lies and ideas about myself that were unintentionally planted by myself as well as others. *Restoring the Foundations* set me free from imprisonment of my mind, emotions, and erroneous expectations. For the first time ever, I felt free to be me.

Application

Maybe not everyone feels the need to go through a healing ministry; however, healing cannot be overlooked. Sometimes, having positive outside perspectives helps us navigate our psyche and innermost struggles much better than we could do on our own. Simply put, we don't know what we don't know. And it is okay to get help. In fact, it is healthy. Any expert in mental or spiritual health would encourage you to allow someone to help you navigate what's inside even when there aren't apparent problems. To illustrate, we should not wait until we're sick to start eating a healthy diet. We should eat a healthy diet to keep our bodies in good working condition to avoid and minimize sickness. It's no different with our minds when it comes to knowing who we are. It should be a consistent and persistent course of action and exercise to keep our minds free from succumbing to the pitfalls of life and thus hindering us from being who we were fully meant to be, and how we are fully meant to lead. Invest in yourself and be consistently intentional about doing so.

For me, after having gone through these two dynamic experiences of the marriage retreat at *JH Outback* and the *Restoring the Foundations* ministry, I felt like a transformed person. I was full of confidence and hope, and I knew what I was about and more of who I was. I approached marriage, parenting, and work differently. But I knew that to sustain that kind of confidence and walk with this new character and identity, I had to remain intentional about doing what it would take to maintain momentum. I journaled, prayed, talked openly and honestly with my wife, set healthy boundaries with work and other obligations, and reminded myself daily of what I had learned and needed to practically walk out each day. I had to develop routines to reinforce who I was and to cultivate a foundation ripe for sustained change.

Those routines will look different for everyone. For example, I am a morning person. This is when I get invigorated for the day. I wake up typically between 5:00 and 5:30 AM, which gives me one and a half to two hours of *me* time before my kids wake up at 7:00 AM and the day starts for all of us. I pray, read, write, and think...pretty much in that order.

It is important that you develop and become intentional with time to get inspired and understand and build on who you are and what you functionally value. If you are a morning person, use that time to begin engineering that space and what you will do. If you are a night person, start with choosing a night or two when you will do something different to invest in who you are instead of binge watching a show from your bed or couch. Then turn that night or two into three, then four, etc.

You don't have to be rigid. Allow room for flexibility. But as you start to develop a good routine, watch how your day starts changing, how your interactions with people begin changing, and how you start to process the world and people around you differently. Sometimes, you may not even notice the changes, but I guarantee that others around you—some of whom you'd least expect—will.

For instance, in my current role at work, I give a lot of presentations. By nature, I am an introverted person and do not like public speaking. I would normally speak timidly in a low tone. One day, after a presentation, someone I would never have expected to hear from said to me, "Hey man, there is something about you. You have confidence and seem so sure of who you are. There is just a pleasantness about you." I was floored. I had not thought to myself before the presentation that I wanted to project confidence and pleasantness so that someone would comment. When I heard this comment, I knew immediately why and what this was. I knew it was due to the transformation I had been experiencing and was reminded that I wanted to lead with confidence, be pleasant, and treat people with value and respect.

There is no better feeling than exuberantly living out your passions and walking in the identity that you're purposely and intentionally both creating and realizing. In this space is where one leads effectively. People say you're not leading if no one is following. I think that is a false idea. You first must lead yourself before you can lead anyone else. When you lead yourself, in whatever way that may be, you are and will, in fact, lead others either away from or toward something.

8

CHARACTER, IDENTITY, AND WHAT WE DO

What we do in life is strongly influenced by the character we've developed and reveals our frame—our structure, constitution, and nature. Character is the mental and moral qualities distinctive to an individual. It is the way people think, feel, and act based on the qualities they possess.

Have you ever made a to-do list? Have you ever made a budget sheet for your money, so you have a financial game plan on a weekly, monthly, and yearly basis? You may be asking what those two things have in common. A to-do list defines the actions you will take with your time. A financial budget defines the actions you will take with your money over a period of time. What we do and how much money we spend are dynamic indicators of character, what we most value, and what we most ascribe worth to, which effectively shape what we identify with and how others perceive that identity.

As I was growing up, I was a huge fan of a well-known actor's cartoon television creation and shows. He gained the respect of so many and was credible. From what you saw of him, you knew the kind of music he loved, some of his values because of his accomplishments, and that he also valued humor as he brought smiles and laughter to millions. He was the kind of guy people knew and loved. He poured his life into all of it. However, when past actions and behaviors came to light in recent years and landed him in prison, it was a shock to say the least. His reputation had been ruined, and how he was seen in the eyes of the public changed.

As I stated earlier in the book, our identity is often built upon our name—what people say about us or what we can do. What people were saying about this actor changed, and what he was allowed to do changed as a result. His name changed. While I don't know this man personally, I can only imagine he wrestled with his identity in some way. The public's view of this actor definitely changed due to what was revealed and how people subsequently identified him.

To further illustrate my point, sometime after he went to prison, I was sitting in the family room of relative's home at a social gathering. The television was on, but no one was really watching it since people were enjoying the food, fun, and fellowship. As I looked around, enjoying a blissful moment of family time and intentionally taking notice of everyone in the room, I also noticed his show flickering across the unwatched screen. Curious, I waited for someone else to take notice just to see their response. Sure enough, someone finally noticed what was on, and I watched as that person's countenance began to change. First, I noticed a long and uneasy stare at the television as the person seemed to wrestle with thoughts and emotions they wanted to articulate. After a few moments, the individual abruptly spoke up loudly, "Oh, I just can't have this on. I cannot stand to watch this. He is terrible..." The person went on to voice their disapproval and dislike...not of the show, but of the actor and the identity they now attached to him.

This man was once viewed as a great and effective leader and a pioneer not only in television, but also in the collegiate sector. However, perceptions about him shifted when his criminal character flaws were revealed. Thus, one can rightly assume that when a person's actions at any point become misaligned with the groundwork he or she has laid in life, with what has been on display for the world to see, that person can swiftly lose credibility. The influence and reach of this actor or any leader in a similar predicament has been stifled and will be difficult, if not impossible, to regain.

Much of our society operates in a way that does not allow room for a lot of forgiveness and grace toward others, especially in corporate America. From birth, we are conditioned to operate and work with the notion and understanding that there is little to no room for error. And in many scenarios, this is good. For example, you do not want an architect to have an error in the design and construction of a building. You expect to walk into a building and not have it collapse. We invest thousands and millions of dollars into ourselves and others to become experts in their respective fields, and rightfully so. As another example, in medicine, you want a medical team on your side that will get it right the first time, and not exactly *practice* medicine on you. However, what I am getting at is that we can project the "perfection" rule to nearly every area of our lives.

We often, many times without conscious thought, project onto individuals in almost every aspect of life and in so many ways the same expectation of *an extremely narrow margin of error or no error* that we would have with business operations and medical institutions. For instance, when you begin your day, you have in your head that you'd rather not have your day and routine interrupted. You'd rather not deal with crying babies...or crying adults. So, when you pass by someone in the hallway as you are headed to your office, you might cordially, but superficially, ask without desiring a response, "Hey, how are you?" What if that person actually stopped you and asked you to listen to them for twenty minutes as they honestly shared how they are doing? Unless your profession has to do with offering therapy and counseling sessions, you'd likely be irritated that your day was inconveniently interrupted. This is now red-flagging in your brain as an error in your day, and your first thought toward that person may be that of repulsion because all you were expecting was, "Hey, doing good, man!" We avoid changing our routines for what we perceive as an inconvenience.

If we are stopped by someone, we'd likely be writhing with impatience to be done as soon as the person begins to speak. We'd likely not want to listen or extend grace. This theoretical encounter illustrates a version of you that is totally and completely self-absorbed; your responses are based completely on how the encounter affects you instead of the needs of another human being.

If you are thinking that what I just described is not you at all, you might be surprised. This is actually quite common behavior and has even been studied in behavioral science. We humans have a tendency to block out certain stimuli in our environment to achieve goals and reach our destination. We target specific tasks and objectives of the day. When we wake up, we are already thinking about what needs to be done. In our attempt to get those things done, we try to avoid extraneous activities that we perceive as irrelevant that take energy, time, and attention away from what we are trying to accomplish. We purposely blind our perception so as to save mental energy.

Stop and think. Have there been times when you have felt like you did not matter to a person? Have you ever felt like you were not listened to by someone and that they did not *really* care what you thought and felt? Have you ever been told you were guilty of making someone else feel this way? A colleague? Someone working under you? Or even a spouse? Ouch! We must be careful not to become disconnected from those around us and those we are trying to lead as we instinctively try to conserve mental energy. An innocent and rather natural instinct, if unchecked, can so easily be perceived by others as coming from someone who is uncaring and dismissive of people.

Actions Reflect Values

Our actions, whether moral, immoral, or amoral, will always serve as the strongest indicators of what we value, what we identify with, and how others will identify and perceive us. This impacts our effectiveness and success as leaders.

Take for instance the story of a person called Jeroboam in the Bible in the book of 1 Kings. I reference this book because it is filled with in-depth stories about ancient kings and leaders that illustrate the kinds of leaders they were, their character, and their effectiveness and influence. We can glean a great deal from analyzing the successes and failures of these historic figures.

In the case of Jeroboam, he led a great multitude of people with great deception out of fear for his own life and because of self-absorbed pride. Just prior to reading about Jeroboam, I was talking with my wife about skills and talents and how they aid us in being successful. But what is it beyond skills and talents that really determines the depth, impact, and duration of that success? I looked for answers to that question in the story of King Jeroboam.

The books of 1 and 2 Kings not only tell us who the kings were, but also give detailed stories of how they ruled and the results of their actions. Many of them have skills and talents similar to people you know in high-level or frontline company positions, but how we use those skill sets and talents, the impact we make, and how long success is sustained varies widely among different individuals. Just picture in your mind two individuals that you would say have similar skill sets and talents, or put another way, qualifications. Now, reflect on the impact those individuals made. Was it skill and talent alone? What really drives the bus is so much more than that. The way a person thinks, feels, and *acts* on the qualities, including skills and talents, he or she possesses makes up their character; this is what directly influences the depth, impact, and duration of success.

When Alethea and I were dating, I of course met her dad and stepmother, David and Jennifer. They are highly educated individuals, are educators themselves, and hold doctorates in their respective fields of study. I consider them to be two of the most generous and compassionate people I have ever met. Upon meeting them, I experienced firsthand their giving and loving hearts toward people and their family. They had planned and paid for their children and grandchildren to have a weekend of fun at Schlitterbahn, and they had paid for me to come as well. I was able to meet Alethea's family all at once, and it was a beautiful experience.

As we all gathered, I could see the love, excitement, and happiness on David's and Jennifer's faces. That first evening, David took out an old-school ice cream maker that you had to hand crank, and we all took turns cranking that thing to make some homemade vanilla ice cream. We had a blast doing it, and we were all working together. I normally have a bit of anxiety meeting that many new people all at once and in such close proximity to one another. However, I felt none of those concerns in this situation because I felt valued, appreciated, and connected.

David and Jennifer had a profound impact on me by causing me to look at myself and ask, *What am I doing? What am I passionate about? How am I treating people? How am I valuing people? How am I leading people?* I immediately connected with them because they had a way of connecting with others that felt neither forced nor false. It was genuine and authentic because they were operating functionally out of what they valued. It was beautiful and attractive. Others also perceive them as generous people, and thus we see a glimpse of what they value.

To this day, their impact on me has only deepened as I have continued to see their generosity and service toward people in action, despite all of life's challenges they have faced. But it was their actions and character that gave me a sense of what they valued.

Take a look at the image below. I refer to this as the identity pyramid. Identity is a question of who you are. This can be found in what you trust, where you see yourself belonging, what you see as your purpose for living, and where you feel competent. Together, those elements form your identity. Once you have established that, everything else is shaped and fashioned from that.

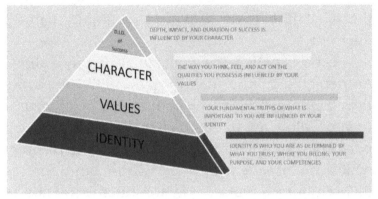

Copyright © Emmitt A. Savannah III – LEADING IDENTITY

Application

Your identity is the foundation of your values—the fundamental truths that are important to you shape your identity. Others may share similar values for sure, but not entirely in the same way or to the same degree of importance as you. For example, many would agree that we value family. However, the ways in which we value our family and demonstrate that are different for each person and involve many factors. Is someone married with kids, married without kids, single with kids, single with no kids, engaged and living with their partner, engaged and not living with their partner, not engaged and living with a partner? A plethora of other situations exist. My point is that the way in which family is valued, and the kinds of values one has and exhibits for family will be different depending on the starting point. It's not that one person will necessarily value family *more* than another, but the way that value is placed on family can be different.

Let's broaden the concept of family values. As depicted in the identity pyramid, values are *your* fundamental truths about what is important to you. Allow me to emphasize the fact that each person's fundamental truths are the lens through which he or she views the world, and that is different for everyone. In fact, fundamental truths for one person may be of complete insignificance to someone else. Have you ever heard the term "perception is reality"? This adage, more righty phrased, is "*Your* perception is *your* reality." I say this a lot to people I train and coach in order to help them approach people and situations with an open mind, with understanding and compassion, and with a more aware and intentional consideration toward others.

Many scholarly journals and articles discuss the mental gymnastics people use to form perceptions and then base reality off of those perceptions. Psychologist Dr. Jim Taylor, Ph.D. said in his article "Perception Is Not Reality," "Our perceptions influence how we focus on, process, remember, interpret, understand, synthesize, decide about, and act on reality."

Perceptions about the world around us, but particularly about ourselves, encase everything about us and how others will see us. Yes, our self-perception has the ability to influence not just how we view everything else, but how others view us. Why? Primarily because of our actions, presentation, and impressions. We act out of our very own perceptions, and the actions are what others see. It is a fundamental truth that perception plays right into identity. Your identity then—found in what you trust, where you belong, your purpose, your competencies—is filtered through your distinct perception of reality and provides the framework for your values, which provide the framework for your character.

Your character is what is more easily visible to everyone else. It's more tangible, more easily identified and definable. Your character is defined by the way you think, feel, and act on the qualities you possess and on the fundamental truths that are important to you. You act on what you value. You value what you identify with. Then when it comes to the matter of success, the depth, the impact, and how long that success is sustained is influenced by a person's character. What this boils down to is that your identity will ultimately determine the depth, impact and duration of your success in life.

Take, for example, the person of Jesus. I know He may be a controversial topic for some, but I am using Jesus as an example of leadership and identity. We know from historical documentation that Jesus knew His identity—what He claimed to be, who He claimed to belong to, and why He was here—by the age of twelve. His values, the fundamental truths of what was important to Him—were reinforced by His identity. There is no recorded account of Him wavering from that. Since He knew His identity and possessed values derived from it, He lived with character traits that reinforced and illustrated His values and identity. His influence reached across thousands of miles of land in just three years, but it reached even farther than that after He was gone. During His last three years on earth, from thirty to thirty-three years of age, He impacted a group of mostly teenagers, whom most people know as the 12 Disciples. Most people believe that all of the disciples, except for one, were well under thirty years old. One betrayed Him because of greed and insecurity, but the others continued influencing other people groups and regions with what they believed in, in what the person of Jesus was purposed to carry out and what He was trying to tell people. The bottom line is this: putting Jesus or any person you know—but most importantly, yourself—in the identity pyramid will lead you to examine and evaluate each step more closely, and will better define success for those placed in it—including yourself. The pyramid will reveal a lot more about an individual than mere skill and qualifications. It's not a black and white analysis, but it really takes into account the entire spectrum of colors of an individual.

Finances and Followship

Though a sensitive and even vulnerable topic for most of us, our financial habits do reveal a lot about us. If you were to let me look at your bank account and transactions, I could start to form revelatory distinctives about your character and what you value to some degree. Show me your to-do list, and I'll learn even more about your character and what you value.

As another example, I follow certain Instagram accounts because I identify with a methodology, a stance, or on a more superficial level, how someone dresses because I have similar style and want new ideas. What or who people follow shows on the most basic level what they like to connect with. Following something or someone, in most cases, means you agree with, like, desire, or wish to emulate actions or thoughts in a like manner; this is associated with your identity.

If a person spent the day reading several books that I have chosen to read, examining my social media accounts and posts, reading my journal entries, meeting my friends, looking at where I've spent my money, and looking through my text messages and browser history, that person would have no problem being able to determine with accuracy what my identity is associated with, how I lead myself, and subsequently how I would lead others.

When it comes to money, our spending truly does highlight what we treasure and value, and what we treasure and value in our hearts are identity indicators. Financial expenditures indicate making a sacrifice to possess what we want and need. It's also true that our desire to accumulate money illustrates something else entirely. So, we must consider both *why* we desire money and *how* we use money. One is an internal transaction (intangible), while the other is an external transaction (tangible).

For example, some may feel that having a certain amount of money provides an inward feeling of satisfaction by giving them a sense of power, control, significance, importance, and maybe happiness. If someone feels this way, what and who they are inclined to follow and listen to will serve them to this end. What they spend money and sacrifice for will also serve them to this end.

We often hear, "*Money* is the root of all evil," but that is an inaccurate quotation of Scripture as well as being taken out of context. What 1 Timothy 6:10 actually says is, "For the *love* of money is a root of all sorts of evil" (emphasis added). Money is a tool and fundamentally neutral. "It is a human invention that sets us apart from the animal kingdom and enables us to subdue the earth by producing from the earth goods and services that bring benefit to others."[2]

I would be naïve to ignore that money is powerful and has much value in our society and world; that has been true for thousands of years. Because of this, we ought to be careful about how we approach money. Several questions will help us discover our motives regarding money and gauge whether our approach to money is healthy. We also need to check how money impacts our relationships and interactions with people who are different than us. I have found these questions to help in establishing healthy financial boundaries:

1. *How does money make me feel when I have it and why?*

    Answering this question will help you establish what transactional relationship money has with the inner you. Some may feel

---

[2] Grudem, Wayne. *Is Money Just a Necessary Evil?* www.thegospelcoalition.org/article/is-money-just-a-necessary-evil/. April 6, 2021.

happy, secure, or quite a bit of anxiety. These money-triggered emotions play into whether our desire for it is inordinate or not, or to the other extreme, if one shies away from money out of an unhealthy fear.

Furthermore, the why answer to this question continues to illustrate to what purpose money serves us personally. Herein lies a core and central value we are serving, often perhaps without realizing it.

2. *How does money make me feel when or if I do not have it, or to clarify even further, when I do not think I have enough of it and why?*

The answer to this question may likely be the exact opposite to the first one. It is exploring in an equal and opposite way the same areas that the first question does.

3. *What do I enjoy spending money on the most?*

The first two questions for the most part tie directly into the third. When you think of having money, you often associate that with what you can or want to get when you have it. This is important to answer for yourself because it identifies what brings you joy. You may not necessarily want a tangible item. It could be an idea or an experience, such as enjoying spending money on a family vacation because you like to travel and have new experiences with your family.

4. *What do I enjoy spending money on the least?*

Knowing this helps bring clarity on another level. Obviously, we have to spend money on both essentials and federal and state government fees; we don't have a choice in those areas, and many understandably do not enjoy paying for those things. But this question is targeting optional spending that you would least enjoy spending money on.

What we register as uncomfortable, unpleasant, and unappealing, we make efforts to avoid and deal with minimally. What we want to avoid also reinforces what we value and devalue.

5. *How much money do I give away—whether to church, charities, non-profits, tips, institutions, or to help a cause or an individual?*

You will notice that I did not ask whether or not you give away money, the reason being that it is a most reasonable thought that you have given away money, whether intentionally or unintentionally. If you truly have never given away any money, ask yourself why not.

The reason I ask how much is because this illustrates a bit of an extension of who we are and what is meaningful to us.

6. *What opportunities has money afforded me?*

Make no mistake about it. We live in a society where money flows through our economy and system and way of operating and living. It's used in the exchange of goods and services.

Looking at how you have used money to attain or obtain something, such as an education and degree(s) that helped you get a job, is nothing bad. It is just a fact of life.

It's important to ask this question because it brings in another angle to our character and values in life. Though it is not a value question, it does provide context into how we view, use, and desire money.

7. *How do I interact with people who make significantly more or less than me? Is there a difference?*

Our society has separated classes of people, tax brackets, and quality of living based on income level. We are constantly bombarded with consumerism, so it for sure makes its way into *how* we personally interact with people to some extent, whether we want it to or not.

Be real with this answer. The reason you should be honest here is because the answer to this question shows how you ascribe value to people.

To make it even easier for you to think through this, pretend you walk into a room full of people where everyone is sitting at tables with people that have the same jobs as them: one table is top executives of a large company; one table has the administrative assistants; another table has custodians; another has frontline staff of a particular department, etc. Based on your *current* role and position, what table do you think you would go to? What would a conversation look like with someone at a different table than yours? Would you sit down at a table that you don't perceive to be "your group" just to talk or would you wave as you briskly walked by?

If you have not taken time to answer these questions, please pause and do that. Understanding more of your identity from a value perspective is crucial. Money—how we use it, why we want it, and what we think about it—is one of the strongest indicators of our value system, and psychologists agree that "money can powerfully influence our thoughts and actions in ways that we're often not aware of, no matter our economic circumstances."[3]

---

[3] Gregoire, Carolyn. *How Money Changes the Way You Think and Feel.* https://greatergood.berkeley.edu, April 9, 2021.

9

TAKE A LOOK AT THE HEART OF YOUR MATTER

In the Bible, Paul, an Apostle of Jesus, reminds believers that because they know God, they have the power of the Holy Spirit to use their bodies in holiness and honor, and the power not to use them in pursuit and acts of lustful passions.

As a person who identifies as a Christian, to use my body in lustful passion is not merely because I *like* to lust. Going deeper, the question I ultimately ask myself is, "What do I perceive that acting in lustful passion does for me that I think God cannot?" I start here because of where I desire to place and draw my identity, which is from God.

Some may think the act of pursuing lustful passions brings an escape from stress because they seek comfort from stressful situations. Or, they feel empowered by acting in this manner to produce a feeling of ecstasy for a few moments. So maybe they like power, either over their situation or over another human being even, which can lead into all sorts of debauchery such as rape, molestation, sex trafficking, or engaging in pornography. Those are all forms of power over another individual for the exhorter's gain.

If you're reading this and you are not a Christian, you may view lustful passions, such as sex and porn, through a different lens than I do. Some might view it as completely natural and a basic human need. But whatever the underlying reason, it is not just a superficial act of doing something. The underlying reason reveals the condition of the heart, or what the person is truly after that in effect, reveals and confirms what they really identify with, whether they will knowingly admit it or not.

The heart—not the physical organ, but more specifically a person's inner self that is made up of the will, mind, thoughts, interests, motivations, emotions, desires, passions, ambitions, and influences—is what shapes someone's life. Have you ever heard the saying, "Out of the heart are the issues of life"? In other words, what we treasure, what our *hearts* place value in, determines what we do. What we do and what we say, what comes out of us that is apparent and evident, speak to what we most value internally, and thus determines how we are identified by others and how we identify ourselves. Luke, a physician and evangelist, and one of the authors of the canonical Gospels, eloquently put it another way in Luke 6:45: "The good man brings good things out of the good treasure of his heart, and the evil man brings evil things out of the evil treasure of his heart. For out of the overflow of the heart, the mouth speaks."

We live in a highly information-driven age. We have so much knowledge at our fingertips. Literally! Even our cell phones give us access to all sorts of information. We are consumers of information and knowledge, constantly bombarded with information, both willingly and unwillingly. We can find podcasts and videos on almost any subject we want to explore and can feed ourselves with it to our fulfillment. We typically take in and make efforts to hold on to what we find helpful, advancing, and advantageous to a cause; and we can simply ignore and forget that which is not. My point is this: The elements we take in, hold on to, or find advantageous to our cause will of course manifest in existential ways.

We are creatures designed to observe the world around us, to learn, and to grow. Much of what we learn, we pursue intentionally, such as going to school to learn a trade and work toward career development, or when we surf the web to find information. We also learn through experiential learning many things that we haven't necessarily pursued. However, the choice is ours to make regarding how we act on what we take in. Take note of what you enjoy learning, experiencing, doing, and pursuing. Also, note what you pursue when no one is watching, whether it is good or bad. My aim is not to bring condemnation on anyone, but to cause you to do sort of a self-analyzation so that you develop a comprehensive picture of who you are, what you're doing, and why you are doing what you're doing. The awareness factor is the starting point for recognizing your identity and then deciding what you will do with this identity awareness: change or remain the same.

Actions and Motives

Leaders' actions alone are not always a foolproof way of deciphering who people are or determining their underlying motives. The same outward actions can be born of different internal motivations. Some are truly altruistic, others are somewhat altruistic in that they serve to benefit and elevate both the leader and the company or others, and some are completely for selfish gain without regard to the well-being of anyone else. A selfish course of action may be overshadowed by seemingly altruistic acts so others are none the wiser, but such actions reveal one aspect of a leader's identity. What we do is indeed a strong indicator of who we are, but why we do something is even more revealing about who we are.

Years ago, a colleague of mine was conducting interviews for an entry-level leadership position. He interviewed many qualified applicants and several had an equal shot at getting the job. Throughout the interview process, the choice came down to two candidates with a strong work ethic. Both were initiators, well-disciplined, and seemingly had all the necessary technical skills, knowledge, and qualifications to do the job well. Nothing stood out that made the selection a sure win for either applicant in my colleague's eyes—at first. On paper, the applicants appeared to be equally qualified, and the choice was proving to be a difficult one. Not knowing what to expect, or even that this question would determine who he selected for the position, my colleague then posed a follow-up question to both candidates: "Should a leader be feared or respected?" One candidate replied fervently that a leader should be *feared.* The other answered, "A leader should be *respected,* but should extend respect and trust to others first." The obvious choice became the person who referenced *respect* and *trust.*

When my colleague related this story, my mouth dropped open in amazement at the difference between the two responses, but I later realized what had happened. This question tapped into the candidates' personal value and character system, and their answers shed light on how the new leadership position would have been handled.

Evidently, the two candidates were influenced by different trusted external factors (where they find identity) that integrated into their personal value system, thereby affecting character that would have inevitably shaped the depth, impact, and duration of success in the leadership position. The identity pyramid was at play here, but also reflective of how not only leaders, but people in all sorts of positions, can mirror each other externally but have different motives. However, inward motives are often just as important as, if not more crucial than, outward performance, especially in cases where inner motives can influence our actions and interactions with others. In this case, one wanted to be feared while the other wanted to extend trust and respect to others. How do you think that would have played out with staff interaction?

Actually, I was the candidate who answered that a leader should extend trust and respect to others first when I was interviewed for the first leadership position I ever held in a corporate setting. From evaluated experiences and observation, I realized that a leader has a responsibility to serve people as well as possible, which functionally supports the needs of the business. One cannot be put above the other, nor can the two be completely separated. The operational success of a company depends on the people. The people function better where they are supported, valued, trusted, and respected.

When I took the StrengthsFinder assessment I mentioned earlier, my number two strength out of the thirty-four provided is that I am an *includer*. As such, I am accepting of others and show awareness and facilitate inclusion of those who feel left out. So, my response to the question was not a forced one. I gave a genuine response out of a place of authenticity because of my values.

The question caused me to realize that my motives weren't something I actively thought about, but a place from which I subconsciously functioned. However, the question about fear and respect allowed me to tap into a default way of functioning and articulate it so that I could understand my own motives.

Application

Sometimes, motives are not known or fully understood by those around us at first. However, those who work closely alongside us or are directly affected by decisions we make will certainly get a glimpse into our motives sooner or later. Interviews are great approaches to expedite insight into a person's motivations. In this situation, the other candidate's underlying approach to leadership was checked in the form of being denied the position. If your ambitions go unchecked by you, they will certainly be checked and perhaps even called out by others at some point, significantly limiting your reach, impact, and success as a leader.

10

SECURITY, BELONGING, AND VALIDATION

As children, we looked up to our parents or whoever had the responsibility of raising us. At the time of this writing, my son Axel is 7, and my son Ellick is 4. They look up to both my wife, Alethea, and me. We are their life support right now. They are growing up in a loving home where they have safety, security, belonging, and reassurance of who they are.

Because they are boys, they tend to play more roughly with me than they do with Alethea. They notice that Dad has more physical features and qualities that they understand and can more easily relate to. They are aware that hitting Mom is way off limits. However, with Dad, they like to wrestle and get rough.

It's crucial to understand that when my boys are wrestling and being superheroes, I have the opportunity to reinforce a part of their identity in those moments. It is more than just wrestling and playing tough. Psychologically, males start to tap into that innate and instinctive sense of being a protector at a young age. This is why boys, in general, are fascinated by superheroes and want to destroy the bad guy. As you might have guessed, I am typically the bad guy they are trying to destroy when we wrestle. Females, on the other hand, begin to tap into an innate and instinctive sense of nurturing at a young age. This is why girls generally like playing with baby dolls.

What my boys see me do, they want to do and imitate. I have the power and authority to show them what they can and cannot do, where they can and cannot go, and ultimately instilling a sense of who they are and giving direction to their identity.

When my family is around people for a length of time, those who know us will pick up on what my boys do or say that reflects either Alethea or me. Why? We are their world and, as such, are reinforcing their identity. They will imitate what they see us do or hear us say because it is from us that they obtain security, belonging, and validation.

Application

As we mature, we never stop looking for that which brings us security, belonging, and validation. As adults, we can surround ourselves with or attach ourselves to those things—whether spouse or significant other; children; material possessions; status; money; recognition and approval; or power within or over something, someone or a group of people. In and of themselves, these things are not necessarily bad. However, the weight and worth that we ascribe to these things is critical because our identities may hinge on these elements without us realizing it.

Take, for example, a door hinged to the wall. Without the hinge, the door will fall to the floor and cease to function. Although it is still a door, it can no longer function as a door. The same can be said of people. What you hinge your identity on is critical. If you hinge your identity to a job then lose the job, what happens to your identity? That's what we should explore and consider. As we move through life, our experiences change, what we agree with and on changes, and what we value changes as well. That is a natural part of life. What also changes is how much power over us we give those things.

Interview

I conducted an interview with an executive-level company leader because I was interested in how some of these ideas play out in the view of someone in that position. I asked nine thought-provoking questions. Though there are no right or

wrong answers, you should ask yourself these
same questions and answer truthfully:

1.   What motivates you as a leader?
2.   How do you define success?
3.   What role does character play in your
     experience and career as a leader and as
     a spouse and a parent?
4.   What have people said about you that
     has affected the way you lead?
5.   What do you believe about yourself that
     has affected the way you lead?
6.   Has there ever been a time when you
     were unsure of yourself as a leader, and
     did others notice?
7.   What brings you a sense of value, worth,
     and security?
8.   What kind of leader would you envision
     yourself to be if those things were taken
     away?
9.   How have your view of yourself, your
     beliefs—whether religious or not—how
     others view you, your namesake and
     your competence affected the way you
     lead?

The leader and friend I interviewed currently
serves as vice president of a department in an
organ and tissue donation organization.
Beginning in an entry level position, he gradually

worked his way up to top leadership and now oversees a department of about fifty people, comprised of different teams. He has worked with grieving families and in many other facets of the industry. With his permission, I am sharing our conversation below.

Question: *What motivates you as a leader?*

Answer: It's a combination of trying to continuously learn and putting that knowledge to work in my staff or in my team. If I learn something that's going to help them, I want to pass that along. I also do want to motivate people. I am trying to grow people constantly. That's kind of the difference between a manager and a leader. I don't know what class I heard this in, but it was something about "managers will get people to do what the manager wants them to do, and a leader will get people to understand and want the same things that the leader wants and will put it on themselves and work towards that." So, if we can convince people that what I want is a good thing, they'll work harder for it than if I tell them they have to do it. [I try to] use that mindset to kind of get people to develop and learn and use new skills. Seeing someone who goes from a new hire to a leader—even if by attitude instead of title—is motivating. You can kind of put your fingerprint on someone like that and then watch them grow. It's definitely motivating.

Question: *How do you define success?*

Answer: Seeing your staff grow is definitely a sign of a good leader. Business wise, if you have a well-run, proactive department, and you're able to develop your staff to a point of where the "this keeps happening, and it's frustrating, and I hate it" mindset changes to "this keeps happening, so how can I fix this?" mindset, your staff will start looking for answers themselves because you foster [the idea] that "it's okay to identify weaknesses in our processes, and you're supported to come up with great ideas, and your ideas are important to me." So, if you can get a staff that's fully involved like that, I think that's kind of a sign of success. Personally, it's trying to do the right thing because it's the right thing, not because it's the easy thing, and doing it the right way, which doesn't necessarily means it's the easy way, but it's the right way. A successful leader is able to identify potential and helps people reach it.

Question: *What role does character play in your experience and career as a leader, and what role does it play as a husband and a father?*

Answer: I think character is one of the most important things across the board, whether in business or at home. I've worked with managers and leaders over me that had high character, and you felt more trust there, and you were able to operate how you thought you should and make mistakes. That's kind of the key. I've had leaders with questionable character, and you never felt comfortable going outside of the parameters of what they wanted. With character, you're going to be doing the right thing consistently because it's right. That works at home as well as it does at work. I think character is kind of hard to define, but everyone sees or recognizes it when it's not there. It's being fair, and helping others, and not needing control to be called a leader—that's not what leaders are; that's what managers are.

Question: *What have people said about you that has affected the way you lead?*

Answer: I heard one thing as a manager that hit me, and I thought, "Well, I guess that's a good thing." The director mentioned to a few people, "Joe doesn't talk a lot at meetings. He doesn't voice his opinion very often, so when he does speak, I pay attention because I know it's something that's important, and he's not just filling the air with his voice. He's communicating something I need to think about or worry about." Some people like to be heard for the sake of being heard. I tend not to be that way. I try to make sure that when I'm talking, especially when it's a "what do you think" question, that I have tried to think through and not just give my first opinion about the situation. In that situation, it was a positive comment, but the same trait can also be viewed as me not having an opinion, which isn't necessarily the case. So, I have tried to change some and speak up a little bit more than I used to. I do continue to work on speaking up sometimes, even when it's not comfortable for me or in my nature to be the first one to talk.

Question: *What do you believe about yourself that's affected the way you lead?*

Answer: I know I don't know everything, and I'm not going to pretend that I do just for the sake of being heard. I think I have a good sense of what's right and wrong, in general, in life. You base some decisions and your attitude toward people and situations on that. I think starting at that point is a good thing. Some things don't come as naturally to me—like being suspect of situations and people, so I have trusted people more than I should, and it's bitten me in the butt a few times. I think I would rather have it that way than the other way around though, where I don't trust people enough and they don't see me as approachable or someone they can talk to, or someone that has their best interest at heart. I think that's kind of key. I tend to see the "glass half full" side of situations.

Question: *Has there ever been a time where you were unsure of yourself as a leader, and did others notice?*

Answer: Coming from a sales position to a new manager role, you are getting a lot of information from above to push out to the team, and you're getting a lot of feedback from the team who don't necessarily agree with the people above you, and you end up being the middle person. Learning to navigate being the messenger for the organization and how that sometimes affects you, but then also trying to make the team work well together [required] learning new skills. My reaction is to tend to try to hold back and figure it out before I start doing. That worked for me in a lot of ways to prevent mistakes, but it also worked against me when I failed to act when I probably should have or didn't act soon enough. Working for someone who is more involved in your daily job, like a micromanager, makes you question your work to the company and your abilities because you don't have that freedom to put your stamp on things and make mistakes. I think that's the biggest difficulty: when you're in a situation where you feel like you can't make a mistake, it's difficult to be an effective leader, because leaders do the best they can, and they don't always get it right. No one does. But if the environment you're in is one where that's it if you make a mistake, then you kind of pull in your arms and don't want to make a mistake and don't act when you probably should. The second part, did others notice: nothing ever got back to me, but I am sure there were times when people felt "he needs to do more" or "he's doing the wrong thing."

Question: *What brings you a sense of value, worth, and security?*

Answer: I think my personality is really trying to put others before myself and look out for others before myself. I don't always get that right. I think value is helping and watching others grow, which validates what I'm able to contribute to their lives and to their growth. I think that's kind of some of the worth too— when you see people grow as a result of your influence or just being in your life, whether it's your kid, or your spouse, or your coworkers or anybody else—if you see the good in you in someone else, it validates your ability. I don't know if that's the best word. You don't do that for accolades. It's really about the transfer of whatever knowledge, perspective, and experience that I have that's good. The value I have is in passing that on; it's kind of the one of the responsibilities I guess everyone probably has—to pass on the good and not the bad. And then security...obviously financial security is important, so there is growing in that area too. It's having the right balance in life. If I feel like I am doing okay in life and at work, then I have security that I am where I am supposed to be and doing both of them well; but when they get out of whack, I can tell when work is taking up too much time or I'm not spending enough time at work. You feel insecure in whatever area you're not spending enough time in. That balance is what gives me the security. When both of them are humming along and I'm doing good, I feel like, "Alright, I'm doing good, this is a good time." When it's not, you start worrying about the other side, usually.

Question: *What kind of leader would you envision yourself to be if those things were taken away?*

Answer: I think I would still want to learn for myself. I would still try to help others grow. If nothing else, just improve my life, my knowledge base, what I am capable of, and try to continuously grow that way. You do have to always be trying to improve yourself so that you are prepared for whatever opportunities you have to be a leader in any area.

Question: *How has your view of yourself, your beliefs—whether religious or not—how others have viewed you, your namesake and your competence affected the way you lead?*

Answer: I think I see myself as a trustworthy and trusting person. I feel that most people know what the right thing is and can recognize it when it's there or not there. I have never been one that needed or wanted recognition. I don't need to be in the morning meetings hearing someone say, "Joe did this great stuff." It's more about watching the team do things. Yes, I have a part in that and that's great, but I don't need the recognition to validate that. As far as religious beliefs, the big thing I kind of take from that and apply across all parts of my life, is just the importance of doing the right thing, or acting right. The importance of grace to everyone. If you mess up, I still can trust you again. It may take some time—nothing is the end of it. People say you find what you look for, so I tend to try to look for the good in people and trust their intentions... and that's what I try to put in all of my life...I also [believe] that I don't need to have all the power, and [I] demonstrate that. It's more powerful to trust that you can give up your power to other people (whether at home or at work) and let them have control over some areas that your position says you have control over. [It's important to give] up some of that power just so you can watch people grow or help people grow, knowing that, just like everyone else, they are going to mess up and learn from it. That's kind of the short answer, I guess.

I truly loved interviewing my friend about this because it provided more insight and a perspective other than my own. As you read his responses, I'm sure that some of what he said resonated with you and some did not. In addition, your answers would likely be entirely different from his because your motivations, values, and what brings you a sense of security, belonging, and validation are influenced by different factors. That is the point I want to make: we all see and evaluate the world around us through different lenses.

In my opinion, the one question that is most critical and foundational is question 7—*What brings you a sense of value, worth, and security?* The reason this is so critical is because the answer illuminates the responses to all the other questions. What you value, what worth you see yourself having, and what makes you feel secure are at the very core of who you are, how you function, what you do, and how you lead yourself and others. They influence how you act and live. Twenty years in the past, your responses in all these areas were likely different than they are now—and most likely something you neither thought about nor fully understood. Twenty years from now, your responses will likely have changed again.

Understanding the answers to these questions can radically shape your life, cause you to change your life, or even maintain the status quo. But if what you value or find worth and security in is thwarted in some way, either by you or someone or something else, where would you aim at that point? Who would you be, really? And even more important, what effect would that have on how you see yourself?

When you do not have a sense of value, security, and belonging, you will have a difficult time adding value to others or convincing them of their worth. If your sense of value, security, and belonging is fickle, you will lead or inspire others the same way. Your approach to work and home life are impacted by these aspects of your identity.

I personally realized my value and worth were coming from what I foolishly thought I had control over. Once that became threatened, I gradually spiraled into a state of depression and mental unrest, and my soul was tormented because of my inability to control and maintain perfection in areas of my life that mattered to me. My identity was wrapped up in what I wanted to control, what I expected to do perfectly but could not. My security, belonging, and validation came from how perfectly I handled my responsibilities in any task or relationship—husband, father, friend, leader and coworker at work, leader and musician at church, son, and brother.

You see, we all carry a variety of titles or positions that have responsibilities attached to them. For me, it was not enough to just have the titles. My identity was directly predicated by how perfectly I functioned in those areas, in either meeting self-expectations or meeting expectations projected onto me by others. Without realizing it, I drew my value and identity from doing both perfectly. When those areas of life started to fall apart, my identity suffered, and I ceased to function in a healthy way.

That does not have to be you. Do not make the mistake of placing your value, security, and belonging in the fleeting things. You will be a fleeting leader. Instead, delve into where you have placed your value, security, and belonging to ensure it is planted in what is certain, proven, and solid. Doing so will produce a certain, proven, and solid leader.

11

PEACE, EXCELLENCE, AND PERFECTION

Some may see themselves as perfectionists, but what does that really connote? The word *perfection* is often equated with excellence; yet when people say they are perfectionists, we breeze over it or perhaps even laugh a little. We typically understand perfectionism to mean that people like to be detailed about what they do to achieve a flawless outcome because this is satisfying to both producers and consumers. Almost all of us can agree that we want things to be done right. However, this idea of excellence and perfection shouldn't be too quickly overlooked, especially for those who would self-classify as perfectionists.

Back in February of 2020, during my morning quiet time of reading, writing, and reflecting, I came across a passage of Scripture in

1 Thessalonians 4:9-18 that resonated with me regarding the idea of where we draw our peace and security and to what degree we do that:

9 Now as to the love of the brothers and sisters, you have no need for anyone to write to you, for you yourselves are taught by God to love one another; 10 for indeed you practice it toward all the brothers and sisters who are in all Macedonia. But we urge you, brothers and sisters, to excel even more, 11 and to make it your ambition to lead a quiet life and attend to your own business and work with your hands, just as we instructed you, 12 so that you will behave properly toward outsiders and not be in any need. 13 But we do not want you to be uninformed, brothers and sisters, about those who are asleep, so that you will not grieve as indeed the rest of mankind do, who have no hope. 14 For if we believe that Jesus died and rose from the dead, so also God will bring with Him those who have fallen asleep through Jesus. 15 For we say this to you by the word of the Lord, that we who are alive and remain until the coming of the Lord will not precede those who have fallen asleep. 16 For the Lord Himself will descend from heaven with a shout, with the voice

> *of the archangel and with the trumpet of God, and the dead in Christ will rise first. 17 Then we who are alive, who remain, will be caught up together with them in the clouds to meet the Lord in the air, and so we will always be with the Lord. 18 Therefore, comfort one another with these words.*

Most would agree that if we lead our lives well, we gain the opportunity to lead others. In 1 Thessalonians 4:9-18, Paul the Apostle, the writer of the passage above, is writing to a group of people in Thessalonica, which is now in northern Greece, who were referred to as the Thessalonians, to remind them they should live peaceful lives, and work and walk properly toward those who were outside so that they may lack nothing.

Peace and excellence are two words that have two different conditions. Peace is a state of being, while excellence is a state of doing, and both can be pursued. People have different motivations for pursuing excellence. For example, I can decide I want to perform with excellence because that brings me peace. I can also decide that I strive only for peace. Excellence involves action, while the other doesn't necessarily have to. Whatever the end goal, both are influenced by something that gives clues about our self-image or our identity.

In most cases, excellence is identified as an achievement or a recognized manner in which we work. Several reasons may exist for why a person wants to be excellent, and that is the question we should ponder. What does being excellent bring to us that defines our purpose, or defines *us*?

Most people do not know how others would answer this deeply personal question. They see only the achievement of excellence and are perhaps drawn to it based on whatever perception of it they have, whatever image or idea to which they are personally aspiring. But what if people did know others' deep and underlying reasons? Would that impact how much more or less people would be influenced to follow someone else, or to what degree they would model a part of their life after another?

I think most would agree that excellence or working with excellence makes sense, and everyone wants someone on their team who performs with excellence. At the end of the day, we'd like to feel like we did an *excellent* job, or that someone we are in charge of did an *excellent* job. We hear this all the time, especially when we praise another person for their efforts and achievements. However, as we lightly toss around this term when giving praise to people or saying we want excellence from people, we should evaluate what we mean by that. Does excellence mean perfection? Or does it mean that the person gave it their best shot, even if it did not quite hit the mark? Would you still say the person did an excellent job even if the goal was not met?

I read an article by a psychologist, Barbara Markway, Ph.D., entitled "Pursuing Excellence, Not Perfection," in which she wrote, "Perfectionists strive for impossible goals. Pursuers of excellence enjoy meeting high standards that are within reach." The article is a great read that will help unpack that quote.

As I reflected on the title and the contents of the article, I was reminded of a pastor and his wife for whom I have great respect. They would often say, "Excellence is doing the best you can with what you have." When I first heard this, I thought that statement was absolutely wrong, because I equated excellence with perfection. I slowly learned this was not the case. At the time, I was a part-time church music director, and as such, I would practice a lot so that when it came time to play for the congregants, it would go smoothly and without a hitch. I expected to never mess up, and I expected the same of everyone else on the team. I expected people to practice and work as much and as hard as I did. However, the truth of the matter was that at times we did mess up. In fact, I messed up a lot. My view of excellence slowly changed over time as a result. I was pouring all I could into delivering something perfect and beautiful, but I rarely walked away after a performance thinking of it as such. I looked at myself as a failure, and I looked at my team as failures at times as well. I was often disappointed and frustrated. I was the hardest on myself because I thought I was not being excellent, because to me, excellence equaled perfection.

All of us on the team had full-time jobs, some were married with children, and some were in school and working. I was working a full-time a job, married with children, and then doing music director responsibilities for the church part-time, so I was easily working a sixty-hour week.

I had reached a breaking point where I began thinking more about the statement, "Excellence is doing the best you can with what you have." I was not a professionally trained musician. I was self-taught, but with an ability and desire to use my gift in the church to honor God. I was unable to work the music director's job full-time. I had a wife and kids, so family was important. I had a full-time job that was also important. My point is that I had a lot going on. Music was a part of this, but I tried to take something to which I could devote only a fraction of my time and make it everything. The delivery of a *perfect* presentation of sound to the congregants became my priority and purpose; and when it went well, I felt complete, whole, validated, secure, and happy. I even felt a greater sense of worth and value. That feeling caused me to expect perfection one hundred percent of the time—which was just not realistic. When a performance did not go perfectly, I was enraged because, deep down, I lost a sense of who I was as it challenged my purpose and identity. I would instantly become grouchy, short-sighted, ill-tempered, and cold with myself and the team. I was even called out on it at times, but I justified my actions because I felt the team needed to do better. That severed my ability to connect and influence. I needed to change, and I needed to do it quickly.

Application

Leaders who identify as perfectionists can have unrealistic goals, both for themselves and for others. It is one thing to have high expectations, but an entirely different thing to demand perfection. You may quickly lose the respect of others because your program becomes more important to you than the people that are working within it. With that said, it is important and worth noting that there are a lot of specialized areas of certain jobs and industries which have zero margin for error, such as flying in an airplane from point A to B. You expect perfect function and operation of the plane because errors here could result in loss of life. Those kinds of high reliability jobs, if not done with a degree of perfection, could have catastrophic results and jeopardize the safety of human life. What I am referring to are activities that, if not done with *perfection,* will not directly impact life or longevity of life. To put it in a more practical way, I am talking about activities which heavily involve interpersonal relationships and working well with others.

In the example I gave of myself as a music director, it was important that I begin asking myself more *why* questions to get to the root of my issue. It's something you can try as well. I am not a psychologist, so I am not going to advocate that this is the best method. I am merely attempting to cause you, the reader, to ask the *why* question behind the what. The series of questions below can be applied to any issue with which you struggle. Just as my answers (in italics below) revealed a part of my identity, the conclusions you draw about yourself in answer to these questions will reveal part of yours.

Question: *Why do I want to be perfect?*

Answer: I want to be perfect because it makes me feel good about myself.

Question: *Why do I want to feel good about myself?*

Answer: I want to feel good about myself because it keeps me positive and motivated.

Question: *Why is it important that I feel positive and motivated?*

Answer: Being positive and motivated means that I am more productive.

Question: *Why is it important to be productive?*

Answer: Being productive means that I complete important tasks responsibly.

Once you have all that, then work backwards using your answers to form the final question.

Final Question: *Since my answers have revealed that I need to be responsible by being productive, which is possible when I am positive and motivated because I feel good about myself when I am perfect, what happens to my view of myself when I am not perfect?*

As you can see, you can continue with the why questions until, at some point along the way, you create a question using all of your answers to find out what happens to your self-image if the answer you ended with is not met.

In order for me to move forward well, I first had to go backward to reveal what was inside, to reveal my motivations, a part of my identity, and attempt to be real and truthful with myself to better understand what it was that I was giving an inordinate amount of worth to that was so attached to my sense of self-worth, self-appreciation, and self-approval. Outwardly, I had a view that others saw me in the same manner, and it brought more and more anxiety. I believe we can all experience this to differing degrees when our view of ourselves is challenged.

The point here is a bit of self-exploration, to discover answers to questions you have probably never asked. It is important to know yourself. When you do, you understand how or why you act in certain ways, and how you are currently influencing others. This is in essence what leadership is—it is largely your influence on others; but, foundationally, it begins with what is influencing you and how you are being influenced to think and act.

12

IDENTITY RESOLUTION

At the end of the day on February 6, 2020, I read a social media comment by a man stating what his life was like living with a wife who suffers from dementia, and my heart sank. I almost did not want to even finish reading what he had written because I was so saddened by what he related; I couldn't begin to imagine what he was going through, but I was so shocked by his resolve at the end of the post. It was not a "woe is me" comment; instead, his heart was revealed through what he wrote. Although he was saddened by his wife's condition, he had retained his joy in life. Who he knew himself to be continued to exist; his identity remained intact. This made a profound impact on me.

The very next morning, I woke up at 4:45 AM. I tossed a bit, trying in vain to go back to sleep, then finally got up and went into the dining room to begin my usual morning routine of journaling, reading the Bible, and reflective writing on God's Word—but that morning was different. I spent that time thinking, reflecting on, and writing about the man who had made the comment on social media. Then I thought a bit about work. I had a deep sense of breakthrough, especially within my department at work, a feeling of accomplishment in several areas. Our team had finally found solutions for a major issue we had been having for years, but that would not have happened if I hadn't striven to bring us all to the table to work together. I sought to bring value to the team by hearing from them, soliciting ideas, and discussing solutions together; and it produced good fruit. The best part is that it was not even my solution that was implemented, but another team member's. That was impactful because I saw myself in a different light and understood even a little better how I did not have to be perfect; I just had to care. That was a realization for me of an identity shift.

After journaling that morning, I felt prompted to start praying and began with two words: "Lord, I..." Then I stopped and began to reflect on God's mercies and grace in my life, how He has embraced me in His arms, saved my life, and given me purpose and identity. I then stopped to read my RTF (*Restoring the Foundations*) generational blessing statements and everything began to clear up for me. RTF is the counselling ministry for individuals or couples that my wife and I went through in the spring of 2019. It provided hope for healing, freedom from life's deepest struggles, and renewed purpose for living by encouraging a personal encounter with God's powerful love, presence, and peace. I typically repeat this statement when speaking the RTF affirmations over myself, and it begins with, "I renounce the sins and curses of (the old detrimental belief I was functioning out of, e.g. fear and control). I break these powers from my life and from the lives of my descendants through the redemptive work of Christ on the cross. I receive God's freedom from these sins and the resulting curses. I receive the blessings of (things like power, love, a sound mind, boldness, light, wisdom, discernment, etc.)." On this particular morning, though, I did not recite what I renounced; I just recited the blessings I had received because I was realizing that what I had been renouncing had been falling off and no longer had a hold on me.

When I went through this RTF ministry, the Lord spoke these blessings to me as I began to receive healing and restoration. I was on a downward spiral, with suicidal thoughts and a wrongly placed sense of purpose and identity. I had complete control of situations and the responsibilities entrusted to me, of what I expected myself to do perfectly; but my world, my identity started falling apart when I could not be perfect in each of those areas that were important to me. That way of living could not sustain me. In fact, it nearly killed me.

The following blessings, believe or not, are words I heard inwardly from outside my realm of understanding that I attribute to God's spoken identity over me and my purpose to which He has called me. I will speak more to that purpose after sharing what those blessings are for me.

I Receive the Blessings of:

Belief, God's voice, truth, freedom, trust, forgiveness, faith, receiving the Father's heart, contentment, peace, joy, rest, assurance, my godly identity, being me, love, son-ship, adoption, being wanted, being welcomed, comfort, provision, a home, God's value of me, His treasure, priceless, precious, one of a kind, freedom, a heart of reconciliation, a warrior—like David (righteous warfare), strength, boldness, courage, a leader, compassion, nurturing, acceptance, direction, redemption, restored honor, robe of righteousness, a new wardrobe, a new beginning, power, a sound mind, light, wisdom, discernment, joy of letting go, freedom to move aside, the blooming presence of the Lord like a bright multi-colored flower, radiant glory of God, I am bending by the Holy Spirit— blowing in the wind, grace, Jesus as my well of water, drinking of the sweetness of the Lord's eternal love, a peaceful home with Him, steadfastness, hope, friendship, financial and spiritual wisdom, financial and spiritual discipline, selflessness, a giving heart, power to walk triumphantly, the finished work on the cross, restored intimacy, purity, and authority.

As I sat just reading and reciting my blessings, I wondered if I were in that man's shoes, with a wife suffering from dementia and our golden years no longer a realistic expectation, would I be able to handle it? Would I throw in the towel? Then I thought about the end of his post. He resolved to place his hope and trust in God and said that the prayers of others would be more powerful and stronger than anything else to sustain him.

I realized that this life was not meant to be lived with selfish thoughts of what I can get out of it, how happy I can be, or being as comfortable as possible by being as perfect as possible. No, I resolved that my life would be lived to glorify God, to make Him known and seen through the life I live. If my wife were to suffer, as hard as it may be, I know now that God has equipped me to live on, care for her, and reflect Him.

Though you may not share this belief, Jesus suffered more than anyone. He carried the weight and effects of sin of the world on His shoulders. Flesh was ripped from His body. If the flesh ripped from mine is my family suffering, so be it. Though it may cause hurt, pain, sadness, and of course giving my all to be there for my family, God will still be glorified in and through that. If the flesh ripped from my body is me losing a limb or going blind or deaf, then so be it. God is glorified. He will be made known, and my life will be lived to that aim and end.

This is my identity. It cannot be taken away—not by losing things of this world, or the death of those close to me like my wife, children, family, friends, etc. It cannot be taken if I lose my job and have to make a career move. My purpose and identity are not wrapped up in that. It cannot be taken when I cannot perform all my responsibilities perfectly and control the outcome of the situation. My job or career path is merely an extension of what I have an ability to *do* while on earth, but it is not a complete picture of my identity. My *doing* does not equate to my *being*.

Where my identity is placed allows me to freely *do* without fear of failure or rejection. We will all fail at something, and we will all face rejection. Identity should not be based on those failures.

If your identity is challenged or taken when failure and rejection come, then your identity is placed in something that can be tossed to and fro like a kite in the wind. When the wind blows with favorable conditions, a kite flies. When there are no favorable conditions, a kite remains on the ground. A kite doesn't stop being a kite just because the wind is not blowing, but so many have this view of themselves. They believe that when they are not in favorable conditions, they mean nothing; their sense of identity is challenged and stripped away. Through loss of status, job, money, a family member, or not having achieved a goal yet, they believe they suddenly stop *being* when they aren't *doing.*

Though it is an over-simplification, no one says about a kite, "This isn't a kite because it's not flying." Similarly, we do not stop being because we aren't doing. Yes, doing is part of our identity in a sense—we do because of what we are. But remember that the definition of identity is found in what we trust, belong to, and our purpose and competence; it's a state of *being* rather than *doing.*

Let's continue with the kite example. We'll call it the identity kite. Let's say the identity kite did have an ability to think, act, and create. The identity kite could say, "I trust in the wind to help lift me because, based on how I am designed, I will fly." So, when the wind comes, it flies. When the wind stops, the kite goes to the ground. It then says, "Even though the wind stops, and I am on the ground, I know who I am. I belong in the family of kites. I can speak to other kites while I am on the ground and let them know who they are as well."

Unlike kites, we are not stagnant and stuck to just one design. We evolve and our mindset can be changed. We conform. Kites do not have this ability. But the point is this: the design of the kite, the way in which it is framed and built, allows for it to fly when there is wind. In the same manner, your frame, how you have been built on the inside, determines how you will fly in life. While a kite must be lifted by the wind, the "winds" that lift a human being won't always be the same. However, what is important to know and ask yourself is this: What is the wind that lifts us? And what will we do if that wind is taken away?

When the wind that lifts us is taken away, what we draw our sense of purpose and identify from is revealed...and leadership is intertwined in identity. We act out of who we see and understand ourselves to be. Though others can see what lifts us, they likely won't have a complete picture of what is happening with us internally when those winds are removed. Only we can know that and come to terms with the outcome of our motivations when the winds that lift us are gone.

No one can ever take my identity from me because of where I have resolved my identity will originate. I am forever changed...I would even say radically changed by that. My identity is not in anything material—not in socioeconomic status, or power, or control, or even fear. The source of my identity cannot be changed by circumstances, death, sickness, disease, or loss of a job. Literally, nothing can shake my identity because it has absolutely nothing to do with the created things of this world. I lead from that knowledge. My leadership is not perfect, and I am not bound to producing perfect things; however, I will still give great attention to detail and work with as much diligence, care, and concern as I can give. This is true of every aspect of my life with home, work, and relationships with people.

This identity source frees me from the shackles of perfection and performance. But it also enables me to move forward, full of passion and enthusiasm, with the qualities and skill required to do what is needed. I have peace in who I am knowing it is not from a place of *doing,* but from a place of *being.*

Can you imagine a lion trying to be anything other than a lion? What if that lion was trying to be a dog and act like a dog, or sound like a dog? He wouldn't be a very effective lion, would he? But as soon as a lion realizes that he is a lion, and not a dog, he does what a lion was designed to do because he fully embraces his identity of *being* a lion.

At this point, whatever identity you have embraced, I hope you have held it up to see it for what it truly is. Can it be taken? Can it be challenged? What would be your state of *being* if it were? How would that affect what you would *do*? Inevitably, how you lead yourself and others comes from your identity.

Self-Publishing
School

NOW IT'S YOUR TURN!

Discover the *exact* three-step blueprint you need to become a best-selling author in as little as three months.

Self-Publishing School helped me, and now I want them to help you with a FREE resource to begin outlining your book!

Even if you're busy, bad at writing, or don't know where to start, you *can* write a best seller and build your best life.

With tools and experience across a variety of niches and professions, Self-Publishing School is the *only* resource you need to take your book to the finish line!

DON'T WAIT!
https://self-publishingschool.com/friend/

Follow the steps on the web page to receive a FREE resource to help you begin writing your book and unlock a discount to get started with Self-Publishing School.

Can You Help?

Thank you for reading my book! I really appreciate your feedback, and I love hearing what you have to say.

I need your input to make the next version of this book and future books even better. Please leave an honest review for me on Amazon, letting me know what you thought of the book.

Thanks so much!
Emmitt A. Savannah III

CPSIA information can be obtained
at www.ICGtesting.com
Printed in the USA
BVHW010929180721
612042BV00022B/223